THE LESBIAN PATH

THE LESBIAN PATH

Edited by Margaret Cruikshank
Revised and Enlarged Edition

Grey Fox Press
San Francisco

Revised and enlarged edition 1985. Third printing 1989.

Cover drawing by Robert Birle, after a silver labyris crafted by Abbey Willowroot.

Library of Congress Cataloging in Publication Data

The Lesbian path.

    Includes bibliographical references.
      1. Lesbians—United States—Biography.
I. Cruikshank, Margaret.
HQ75.3.L475   1985   306.7'663'0922   85-12519
ISBN 0-912516-96-8 (pbk.)

Printed in the United States of America.

Distributed by Subterranean Company, P.O. Box 10233, Eugene, OR 97440.

For the Minnesota lesbians
whose stories inspired me
to make this book.

CONTENTS

Preface to the New Edition   ix

Introduction   xi

Ruth Baetz: I See My First Lesbian   3

Mitzi Simmons: For You . . . For Us   7

Judy Grahn: *Romeo and Juliet* Replayed   15

Cathie Nelson: A Flower for Judith   19

Matile Poor: A Loving Friendship   26

Jane Gurko: Coming Out in Berkeley, 1967   30

Joan Nestle: An Old Story   37

Margaret Sloan-Hunter: Two Poems   40

Beth Brant: Ride the Turtle's Back   43

Ida VSW Red: Naming   44

Jeanne Cordova: Trauma in the Heterosexual Zone   52

Margaret Cruikshank: A Slice of My Life   58

Monika Kehoe: The One That Got Away   64

Pat Parker: Goat Child   68

Nancy E. Krody: On Being a Lesbian Christian   78

Susan Madden: On Keeping Ourselves Down   84

Maree Martin: Fifteen Years Ago   89

Caroline Ferguson: A Long Struggle   94

Sandy Boucher: Three Stories   100

Nancy Manahan: Lesbian Books: A Long Search   103

Susan Griffin: Silences   110

Margaret Cruikshank: A Conversation with May Sarton 115

Minnie Bruce Pratt: In Which I Weep Like Niobe 125

Sharon E. Budd: Proud Lesbian Motherhood 131

DPat Mattie: No Name He Can Say 138

Del Martin & Phyllis Lyon: Anniversary 143

Monika Kehoe: An Incident in the Fifties 147

Audre Lorde: Of Sisters and Secrets 151

Judith McDaniel: My Life as the Only Lesbian Professor 160

Alix Dobkin: Lavender Jane Loves Women 166

Barbara Grier: The Garden Variety Lesbian 171

Elsa Gidlow: France 175

Jane Rule: Leave Taking 182

Barbara Lightner: O! We Are Just Begun! 190

Rosemary Curb: "Remember the Future" 197

Judith Niemi: Hudson Bay Journal 203

Notes on Contributors 214

Preface to the New Edition

The publishing history of *The Lesbian Path* began in the spring of 1979 when the manuscript was accepted by a small press in Monterey which published it in February of 1980. After some lively disputes with the publisher, who had wanted to call the book *The Love Game on Lesbos*, I regained the rights in 1981. (The early history of *The Lesbian Path* is recorded in correspondence and tapes held by the Lesbian Herstory Archives in New York.) "Self publish or perish" was a popular feminist slogan that year. With a new cover but no change in its contents, *The Lesbian Path* began a new life in June 1981 when Naiad Press became its distributor. Giovanni's Room sold it overseas.

Not long after *The Lesbian Path* went out of print in the fall of 1984, Grey Fox Press agreed to bring out a new edition. For this edition I have dropped several of the shorter essays from the original *Path* and added new work by Jane Rule, Judy Grahn, Elsa Gidlow, and Beth Brant, and an interview with May Sarton.

At the time *The Lesbian Path* was first published, only a few autobiographical articles by lesbians had appeared in print. The situation is very different now: a few full-length autobiographies and several anthologies show our diverse experiences. Public attitudes have not greatly changed in five years, however, and the autobiographical essay will no doubt remain a particularly important form for lesbians to explore. Whatever literary significance our stories hold, announcing our existence is still a political act.

Acknowledgments

For comments on this book in all of its stages I owe special thanks to Nancy Manahan, co-editor of *Lesbian Nuns: Breaking Silence*. I also thank Barbara Grier of Naiad Press for distributing *The Lesbian Path* from 1981 to 1984 and Don Allen of Grey Fox Press for help in revising the book.

Permissions

For permission to reprint articles in this book, I wish to thank the following: Jeanne Cordova for "Trauma in the Heterosexual Zone," which appeared in *Sexism: It's a Nasty Affair*; Sandy Boucher and Susan Griffin for the Modern Language Association speeches first published by *Sinister Wisdom*; Minnie Bruce Pratt for "In Which I Weep Like Niobe," also in *Sinister Wisdom*; Pat Parker for "Goat Child," one of the poems in *Movement in Black*, published by Diana Press; Barbara Lightner for "O! We Are Just Begun!", which originally appeared in *So's Your Old Lady*; DPat Mattie for "No Name He Can Say," published in *Christopher Street*; *Mother Jones* for the article "Lesbian Books: A long Search" by Nancy Manahan (Nancy M. Ruthchild); Druid Heights Books and Booklegger Press for the chapter from Elsa Gidlow's autobiography *Elsa: I Come with My Songs*; Beacon Press for an excerpt from Judy Grahn's *Another Mother Tongue* (copyright 1984 by Judy Grahn; reprinted by permission of Beacon Press); Firebrand Press for Beth Brant's poem "Ride the Turtle's Back" (copyright 1985 by Beth Brant, reprinted by permission of Firebrand Press); *Frontiers* for my essay "A Slice of Life," which appeared in a slightly different form in *Focus*, and *The Advocate* for my interview with May Sarton, which is reprinted with permission from *The Advocate* for August 18, 1983 (copyright 1983 by Liberation Publications).

The articles by Minnie Bruce Pratt, DPat Mattie, and Barbara Lightner were originally written for *The Lesbian Path*.

Margaret Cruikshank, 1985

Introduction

This collection would not be possible without the women's movement, which has helped us find each other, come out, and give positive meanings to that word we used to fear—"lesbian." Within the new women's culture, the flowering of lesbian writing has been especially dramatic because, until recently, so many of us were in hiding. Although books by and about lesbians appeared before the 1970's, they were too few, too isolated, and too furtive to establish lesbian writing as a distinct genre. Now not only are we visible; we are writing about ourselves.

The Lesbian Path, the first book made up entirely of short personal narratives by lesbians, is one work which marks the beginning of our literary expression. Illustrating our quest for new self images, it is a collective work—the autobiography not of one woman but many. This book celebrates the survival of an oppressed group by showing our strength and resilience. Every one of us represented in the anthology grew up in the silence enshrouding lesbianism, a silence which, if broken at all, was broken by lies. Since we never heard of women loving women, we thought we were the only ones who did. Remembering our isolation and believing that this book, if it had existed in the 1950's or 1960's, would have made our self-discoveries less painful, we are naturally eager to record something of our lives. And, like other women who have begun to observe themselves, we have an exhilarating sense of our power to say—sometimes tentatively—who we are.

I began thinking of this book in 1975 in Minneapolis. For the first time, I had a circle of lesbian friends and thus could hear my first stories of lesbians' lives. I started to collect articles in the next two years, when I was the closeted head of a women's studies program at a large state university in Minnesota. I wanted my students to have the book I never had: true stories of strong, women-identified women. The main idea of the collection was to show the diversity of lesbians: women who came out as teenagers, those who found their identities later in life, beginning writers, established writers, women of color, formerly married women, professional women, working class women, those whose sexual preference carried no penalties, and those who were victims of anti-homosexual persecution.

The Lesbian Path did not grow into a book with that rich-
ness—white women and middle-class women are overrep-
resented here, as well as academics and former nuns—but we
can look forward to whole anthologies devoted to the personal
experiences of women of color, working-class women, older
women, and others who represent a minority within a minority.

Also, it hardly seems necessary in 1979 to prove that lesbians
are a diverse group. But perhaps none of us can fully appreciate
our diversity until hundreds of our personal narratives are published: coming out stories, interviews, histories of friendship
networks, material from Lesbian Herstory Archives, and accounts of lesbians in places where we have always been numerous: in sports, convents, colleges, the military and the girl
scouts. The Lesbian Path is only a start; for every story here,
there are thousands not yet written, and tens of thousands not
yet spoken.

THE LESBIAN PATH

RUTH BAETZ

I See My First Lesbian

"We have guest speakers for today's class: two lesbians will speak to us about the place of lesbian women in American society."

What?

My heart pounds out an alarm signal and rushes it through my body. My pupils dilate, my breathing stops and my muscles hold my body at attention. It is 1972, and after three years of college I have come to expect dull classes; this announcement is a shock.

Can the other students see me trembling? Do they notice my pale face and my staring eyes? I am very glad to be in the last row, hidden by the woman sitting in front of me. I hold onto my desk to steady myself. I certainly don't want to do anything silly like fall out of my chair. Oh no. Please let me get through this class without making a fool of myself. Please let me seem like just any other student, intellectually interested and mildly curious.

As the women step to the center of the semi-circle, the words "two lesbians" sink into my consciousness. Not only are they lesbians, but they admit they are lesbians to fifteen strangers! How can they possibly do that? Why aren't they terrified and ashamed?

I begin to scrutinize the two women, searching for any clues of abnormality or neuroses. Do they have any strange gestures or hidden physical deformities? Are they trying to be like men? No. They look perfectly normal. I can see how one of them could be a lesbian, though. She's short, fat, and frumpy-looking with ratty hair and sloppy overalls. It's probably a good thing she is a lesbian; she'd never catch a man. But sloppiness is hardly a sign of abnormality around this campus, and if anything these two women seem more composed and self-assured than the average co-ed. In fact, the other woman is absolutely beautiful. I feel myself staring at her: shiny sun-streaked blond hair, large green cat eyes, soft peach blouse accentuating her lovely figure. How can she be a lesbian? She could certainly get any man she wants; why has she chosen this?

She speaks clearly and confidently, and as I tune into what she's saying I feel my body relax. She's telling of the 1969 Stonewall riots and the way gay life used to be. Whew. I can certainly maintain my composure through this. It's just a history lesson, and I have had enough experience sitting through academic lectures to know that no responses will be expected of me. She speaks of gay bars and of lesbians in the women's movement. She says that gay people need to organize to protest the discrimination against them.

Protest. I feel my body stiffen slightly. My years at U.C. Santa Barbara have been nothing but protests, and people wanting me to join this political group or come to that rally. Is that what it's like to be a lesbian? Does it mean marches and rallies and protests and strikes? Is it a life of constant political struggle? A part of me recognizes the disappointment I feel at this description, but mostly I am relieved that the discussion is about impersonal facts and events.

In fifteen minutes she's finished talking. "Are there any questions?" she asks.

Oh no. The level of tension in my body immediately steps up. I hope someone can think of something to ask. It would be horrible if these brave women came all the way to this class and then nobody was even interested enough to ask them anything. Please somebody say something. A woman raises her hand.

"How did you first realize that you were a lesbian?"

Oh my God. My heart lurches. I see the speaker waver for a split second. Will she come down off the relatively safe intellectual plane and share her life with us?

"I've known for a long time that I was different," she replies. "In high school I wasn't interested in dating boys at all, but I have always had really close women friends." Wow. She knew she was a lesbian that long ago. How can she know herself so well? When I was in high school, dating boys was the only activity and the only topic of conversation; I never questioned its importance. I dated men even in my first years of college, still searching for "the one."

The girl next to me raises her hand. "I can really identify with what you're saying," she says. "I have always felt much closer to women than to men, and really treasured my women friends. It just seems to be so much easier to relate to women, to communicate on a deep level." I look at her. How could she have said that? How could she have risked sounding like a lesbian? A glitter on her finger catches my eye and I see that perhaps she's not so brave after all; she wears an engagement ring.

But other women in the class chime in now too, and soon everyone is talking about their close women friends and how they love the depth and honesty in relationships with women. Why can't I speak? Why can't I raise my hand and say, "I too love a woman and it's the most beautiful thing in my life?" Why can't I stop trembling? My hand threatens to fly up against my will to force the pronouncement, to force me to speak about my life with pride.

I have lost track of the discussion in the throes of my own internal battle. The lesbians have talked about their lives as lesbians, and the women in the class have been open about their affections for women friends. Suddenly it is over. What? People are stirring and organizing their papers to leave. The teacher is making a few wrap-up comments. Oh wait, people, wait. I haven't told you how much I love Maria, or what a wonderful life we have together, or how very lucky I feel to be with her, or how much you're all missing by being with men. People are getting up to leave. My insides are screaming. The people are leaving. My golden opportunity to come out of hiding. My one chance to be proud of my life and my choice.

It's too late. Nearly everyone has left now. I have to pick up my books and look unaffected. Now is no time to break down and give away my feelings, to show my trembling. I walk out of the classroom slowly, slipping back into the whirling mass of students racing to their next classes. I am alone.

I can't remember the rest of that day at all. I know that my mind was reeling for weeks afterwards, and that my body could hardly contain my warring feelings. Did I tell my love about my class? Did I tell her that we might be lesbians? I don't remember. Although we had said our private marriage vows to each other a year before, and my feelings toward Maria were certainly similar to the feelings described by the two speakers in the class, I just couldn't imagine us as lesbians. I had always felt that I was in love with a person who just happened to be a woman. I certainly didn't think I loved her *because* she was a woman. I hadn't known I was different in high school, and I certainly couldn't see myself ever joining a protest or walking down the street with a sign proclaiming to all the world that I was a lesbian. The very thought terrified me.

As the days passed my fears gradually subsided, and I easily slipped back into feeling safe and warm in the arms of the woman I loved. A year and a half later, when we actually met our first lesbian friends, we still avoided confronting our identities, suspecting that we and our new friends were somehow "different" from those weird lesbians out there somewhere.

It wasn't until four years after that sociology class that I really had to come to grips with my identity as a woman-loving woman. First I had to be divorced by Maria and thrown out into the heterosexual world alone. Only then did I actually seek out other lesbians and find that they were indeed normal, just like the women who came to my sociology class, just like me.

MITZI SIMMONS

For You ... For Us

I love her. I feel an intense desire to be close to her. I want to share my feelings with her. I must tell her. No, no, I can't. Impossible. A voice inside me says these beautiful feelings, for which I have no name, are wrong. . . .

Memories flash through my mind: walking together, cooking hotdogs over the campfire at the railroad trestle, playing our guitars in my room. No, the friendship is much too valuable to risk losing; I've never been so close to anyone before. Annie entered my life when I was lonely and too scared to open up myself and my feelings to other people. She came to me with patience and understanding, and with a loving hand she reached inside my heart and gently she let my feelings flow. I can't lose her now; I can't. I would die inside. But what about these feelings that wrack my body with an intensity that I never dreamed possible? They won't go away. Maybe, just maybe, she feels the same way.

"... and when I get married, you can be a bridesmaid in my wedding." A bridesmaid! Doesn't she understand that I want to spend my entire life with her? Doesn't she know how much she means to me? No . . . she doesn't know. She'll never know. Because I can't possibly risk losing her completely by telling her.

The months go by. It's Easter now, and I've been repressing my feelings for Annie for what seems to be an eternity. Although I've tried to tell her how deeply I love her, I haven't attempted to describe all of my feelings to her, for I can't even describe them to myself. There is no name for what I feel; no words can fully encompass my deep love for this beautiful woman. And I can't explain why I long to be physically close to her. It's not just something physical; it's spiritual and emotional and mystical. Could I be in love with her? No, a woman cannot possibly fall in love with another woman. I've never even heard of that; the idea is absurd. But I'm only sixteen years old, and I've never been in love before, so how do I know that I'm not in love now?

Annie and I exchange Easter cards, and we chuckle as we realize that we've picked out the same card for each other. As we read the tender messages of love on them, however, both of us are swept into a mood of deep reflection, and both of us are nearly moved to tears. And then before I know what is happening, Annie is holding me in her arms. I am close to her at last, feeling her warm softness against me, and as we hug each other I realize that with this embrace we declare not only our friendship, but all levels of our love. "Do you know how long I've wanted to do this?" I ask with tears in my eyes. We hold each other again, and as Annie tells me that she was afraid to hug me, afraid that I wouldn't reciprocate her feelings, I wonder to myself if I ever would have found the courage to take that step if she had not.

Our paradise has one flaw—our knowledge that we must hide our love from our parents, our families, our friends, from everybody. We have not yet begun to question the goodness of our feelings, but we have never before witnessed a relationship such as ours between two persons of the same sex, and we know somehow that others would not understand. This knowledge itself is only semi-conscious, but it is there. So often we reach out to touch each other behind closed doors only to jump at the sound of footsteps, fearing that the door will suddenly swing open and that somebody will find out. Loving each other so deeply, we are happy, but we are also scared. Very scared.

And then suddenly it happens. Our world begins crumbling around us, and we haven't time to recover from one blow before another hits us and knocks us down again. Spending the night together at my house, Annie and I are awakened, lying in each other's arms, by the sound of someone opening the bedroom door and then hurriedly shutting it again; Annie's mother finds and reads a love letter that I have written to her; rumors start at school. As a result, Annie and I find ourselves confronted by what are perhaps the most dreadful and terrifying words we have ever heard in our lives—lesbian, homosexual, queer. We don't know what these words mean, but from the way people say them, we know that they mean something horrible and evil. We hear people roll them off their tongues as though they mean some sinful and abhorred perversion or disease—and they are directing these terrible words at us! For a time we ignore the words, but they gnaw away at us inside until we have to know. Using the dictionary to discover that a lesbian is "a female homosexual," we flip to the definition of homosexuality, "sexual desire for others of one's own sex." At this point Annie and I encounter some problems with semantics. Having never before considered the word "sex" to refer to anything other than physical activity between a male and a female, we are confused by the very definition itself. Attempting to apply the label to ourselves creates even more confusion. Are these beautiful feelings that we have for each other "sexual desire"? It is true that we enjoy being physically close to each other, but we are much more deeply involved with each other emotionally than we are physically. Sexual desire? We call it love, and our physical intimacy is simply an expression of that love. Is that the same thing as sexual desire?

Annie and I go to the library in search of more information on homosexuality. We are relieved by what we find. Homosexuals are promiscuous; they are sexually perverted, and they molest young children. Those definitions certainly don't fit us! Our relief is only temporary, however. Why do other people think such terrible things about us simply because we love each other? A memory slowly creeps into my mind, a memory that I have been trying to suppress, of a conversation between my sister and myself that took place several months before I even met Annie. "One of my friends asked me today if you were a lesbian," my sister had remarked to me casually one evening.

"Oh. What did you tell her?"

"I told her, 'No.' " And then after a pause, "You're not, are you?" I didn't think much about the incident at the time, especially since I didn't have the faintest idea of what she was talking about, but now it really bothers me. Why do people think these things about me? And what provoked my sister's friend to ask such a question before I even knew Annie?

As time goes on, it becomes increasingly difficult for Annie and me to convince ourselves that we are not lesbians. My sister, who walked in on us that morning when we were sleeping in each other's arms, has since been making rude remarks to me about our "gross" and "perverted" relationship, and Annie's parents have been confronting her with questions about homosexuality. As we slowly come to accept the label ourselves, we sink deeper and deeper into guilt and self-hatred. We withdraw from our friends because we are afraid to be honest with them;

we cannot go to our parents, knowing that they wouldn't understand. There is no one to turn to.

Annie and I are drowning in a whirlpool of guilt, anguish, self-hatred, and shame. Making our turmoil even harder to bear is the confusion. Isn't the sex of the person with whom one falls in love irrelevant? We are spinning in endless circles; we are getting nowhere. Finally we reach out to a close friend, a person whom we admire, a person who might be able to understand. And even if she doesn't, we trust that she will help us or at least explain to us why our love is wrong.

We are sitting on the steps together, the three of us, and as Annie starts talking I actually believe that I can go through with it. But suddenly I panic. What if she doesn't understand? What if she tells us that our love is wrong? My heart is pounding against my rib cage; the sweat pours my sides. I want to die. I hang my head in shame. "Annie, I don't think I want to go through with this," I cry out, interrupting her when she's barely begun. Annie stops talking and looks at me. Our friend looks at me. I cannot look back. And then a voice reaches my ears as if from a thousand miles away, a soft and soothing voice, the voice of our friend.

"It's all right, Mitzi. I know what you want to talk to me about, and it's all right." I raise my head and stare at her, dumbfounded. "It's all right," she says again. "Really."

Healing takes a long time. Annie and I find other friends we can talk to, friends who accept us, help us, and understand. We are given books that expose us to our first positive view of lesbianism, and we withdraw to read them, to lick our wounds, to become whole again. Confrontations with our parents are increasing now, but our growing strength and belief in the validity of our love enables us to stand up against the attacks and even in some cases to fight back. What once was shame is now turning into pride; what once was guilt turned inward is now becoming anger directed outward.

"Are you and Annie . . . that way?" my mother asks me one day.

"What way?" I return stubbornly, annoyed by her refusal to even speak the word.

"Well, you know."

"No, I don't know."

"Are you . . . lesbians?" There, she finally said it!

"Yes, we love each other."

"Well, I don't understand that at all."

"What's so hard to understand?"

"I don't see what two women can possibly do in bed together," she replies, reducing a very complex, loving relationship to sex. "What DO you do in bed?" Embarrassed and stunned by such an invasion of my privacy, I say nothing at first. Then she is caught in the flood of my anger.

"What the hell do you mean, asking me a question like that? I don't ask you what you and Dad do in bed together!"

Time goes on. In anguish, Annie tells me that her parents are determined to keep us apart throughout the summer. All we have is each other, and we don't know how we can possibly make it through three months alone. But we have to.

As the days of isolation drag on, I spend more and more time reading gay and feminist literature. I hurt from the absence of my lover, but I am quickly beginning to realize that I am not at all alone in my suffering; there are millions of other homosexuals out there, somewhere, enduring pain and injustice because of society's inability or refusal to understand. As my political consciousness grows, my anger grows, too. I see heterosexual couples walking arm-in-arm through the park, and I grow envious and angry because I must hide and continually be on guard like some hunted animal. I watch a tender and moving love story at the movie theater, and I grow more envious and angry because such stories are never written for gays. I watch a heterosexual couple joyfully leaving the church after their wedding, and my envy and anger grow still more intense because I have just read in the newspaper about two lesbians who were arrested in Chicago when they applied for a marriage license! My anger has almost grown to the level of outright hatred before I realize that I am placing blame where it doesn't belong. These heterosexual people believe that homosexuality is wrong for the same reason I once feared my love for Annie to be wrong— they were taught to believe so. They have grown up believing so, and it will take patience and understanding—and openness—on my part before they can come to understand me.

EDIRP YAG. I read the letters of my T-shirt backwards in the rearview mirror as I sit parked across the street from the high school. This is it, the first day of my senior year, my first experience with publicly coming out, and I'm scared. What the hell am I doing? Risking expulsion? Risking my future? No, I'm gaining it. Taking a deep breath, I leave the security of the car, walk briskly across the parking lot, and enter the jungle of students.

Half surprised at not being verbally attacked after walking through the door, I stop for a moment to reflect. I have no idea what to expect, from others or from myself, but I am no longer afraid. Currents of strength surge rhythmically through me; my heart swells with pride. I walk down the corridor, head up, shoulders back, reflecting my triumph in the light of my smile as I cast a forceful gaze into the eyes of each person I meet. Yes, I am gay; the rumors were right, and I'm proud of it! I feel the currents of wholeness, and I know that I will never let go of my self again.

Suddenly I stop, puzzled. Something is different in a way that I hadn't expected at all. Their eyes, once icy cold, now melt away from the fire in my own. Laughingly I wonder at how such situations can completely reverse themselves, shifting from one extreme to the opposite. Was it only yesterday that my eyes could not meet theirs?

I walk into English class and sit down at a table at Annie's side. As the other students rise to move elsewhere, I chuckle softly to myself. My problem? No, theirs. Now I can laugh at experiences that once made me cry.

I am free from guilt, but fear returns. Throughout the year Annie and I struggle to raise the consciousness of our peers by beginning class discussions on homosexuality, and always, the fear stays with me—the dry tightness of my throat becoming cotton, the uneasiness in my voice—because they laugh. Because Annie and I are the only two gay people we know in a school of eight hundred students. Because we are fighting together, but alone. Yet the triumph I feel after speaking out makes it worthwhile.

And we do find support, or at least some objectivity, intermingled with prejudice. When our government class plays Senate in an exercise to help students better understand the legislative process, Annie and I submit a bill guaranteeing human rights for gays. The students come within one vote of passing the ordinance, and the teacher gives us warm encouragement for defending our beliefs. But other teachers close their minds completely. While my economics instructor lectures about the economic impact of discrimination against women and racial minorities, I comment on discrimination against gays. Threatened by homosexuality, he calls me a freak, and orders me never to mention the subject again in his class. I refuse, and anger burns between us throughout the year. The assistant principal is even less tolerant. Knowing that Annie and I are guidance office assistants together, he tells the guidance counselor one afternoon, "I don't want Mitzi and Annie making out on the couch in your outer office."

"Making out?" she replies incredulously. "All they do is talk and study."

"Oh, sure. I know what goes on down there."

Interactions such as these soon convert my fear, like my guilt before it, into anger. I become more bold in confrontations with both students and teachers, and the absurdity of their misconceptions is so great that even as they laugh at me, I am laughing back at them. "The ideal sexual relationship is naturally heterosexual," drones my psychology teacher during a class discussion of homosexuality.

"How do you know?" I shoot back. "Have you ever had sex with a man?"

"Well . . . uh, no," he stutters, obviously embarrassed. "But the male and female bodies complement each other to give greater satisfaction."

"And I could just as easily say that gay sex is more satisfying than straight sex because a man can't know how a woman feels as well as another woman can, and vice versa. But I'm not saying that. Because the important thing is the quality of the relationship between the two individuals. Being gay, like being straight or being anything in between, means more than just sex."

More than just sex . . . Why can't they understand that? Why? Sometimes I want to grab them by the shoulders and shake them and make them understand. Even my own mother, when asking about my relationship with Annie, asked me what we do in bed. And now I see our relationship crumbling. While declaring our personal life has strengthened our pride and belief in ourselves, Annie and I have also felt its harmful effects. We are growing apart, and although our political activism is not solely responsible, it has undoubtedly played a big part. I find it harder and harder to touch her. Whenever we are intimate with each other, I feel as if we're trying to make love in an arena full of people, and I can't do it. I can't distance myself from the situation; it has become too political. It's almost as if the whole world is watching us, as if we've lost all our privacy. And I can't get away from them enough to be alone with her.

And the memories haunt me still. Bits and pieces out of context filter into my consciousness from that ancient, far-away epoch, as close in time as yesterday, one-and-a-half years ago. I don't want to remember. I am strong and proud for what I've experienced, but the memories are laced with pain; and the goodness of the past, the sweet beauty of the times that Annie and I once shared, is lost to me, buried beneath the tears I have yet to cry.

But here—at college, away from the town that my parents called my home—I find peace at last, a beautiful, supportive women's community, and friends. I feel warm energy radiating from them and I lovingly return it with a strong and gladdened soul. The healing is not finished, though. And there's the anger to deal with, anger for having to wait so long, anger because gay people are waiting still. But waiting is not the answer. I write this because I want to ease the suffering of other lesbians and gay men and because I want heterosexuals to understand. And if what I say benefits even one person, my struggle will have been worthwhile.

JUDY GRAHN

Romeo and Juliet Replayed*

Good-night, good-night! parting is such sweet sorrow
That I shall say good-night till it be morrow.
Sleep dwell upon thine eyes, peace in thy breast!
Would I were sleep and peace, so sweet to rest!

In 1954 a peculiar, small, Levi-clad figure strode boldly along
the silent streets of a small class-bound southwestern town,
reciting Shakespeare in a loud voice and plainly ready for any
mischief. At fourteen I was ready to move on to more exciting
body contact than holding sweating hands, hoping Pamela felt
more than some girlish crush. I wanted to kiss Pamela, who
had by her actions, or rather her lack of negative actions, led
me to believe she liked me a lot, and I thought I had found a
foolproof method of bringing up the subject of kissing in a
nonthreatening manner. Shakespeare! Literature! Shakespeare
was going to help me kiss Pamela. Oh good for you, Shakespeare.
It happened that both Pamela and I were invited to a timely
sleepover party at the house of her best friend, Jo Ellen. Riding
merrily to Jo Ellen's house on my trusty blue bicycle, with a
hard-earned copy of *Romeo and Juliet* in my back pocket, I was
very disappointed to arrive and learn that Pamela's mother had
not allowed her to come. And no one else had been invited.
Oh no. All my scheming and rehearsals would be for nothing
unless—did I dare? Did I dare to try to kiss Jo Ellen? Did I even
want to kiss Jo Ellen? She was so crazy. You could never tell
what she would do. But so what? I would try it.

Jo Ellen was a strange person, extremely thin and anemic to
the point of translucence. She did not exactly move, she flitted
in a sideways direction and then abruptly came to rest. She had
boyish bushy hair and was very nervous. Both she and Pamela
were under increasing pressure to be respectable, to be on display at the country club, to prepare to take a highly regulated
place among the elite of the town. What was a horsey crooked-

---

*From *Another Mother Tongue* (Boston: Beacon Press, 1984).

toothed character like me doing at her house? I didn't know. She had invited me. Now she lay stiffly beside me in a sleeping bag stretched out on the floor of her parents' garage. I was reading *Romeo and Juliet* to her by flashlight and asking if she wanted to read a scene with me. She did, and I had it carefully prepared and marked, a scene in which Romeo kisses Juliet. First we just read the lines out loud, and that went fine. Then I suggested we do it again, only this time, I said, "We could act out the actions."

"OK," she said.

"And when we get to the part where Romeo kisses Juliet, Romeo will kiss Juliet," I said.

"OK," she said.

"OK," I said, "I'll be Romeo."

"OK," she said. She lay perfectly still on her back. This made me terribly uneasy because of its similarity to the joke in *Romeo and Juliet* about Juliet spending a lot of her time on her back once she was married, a joke I hated. Why did being married involve lying on the back, I wondered in horror. It sounded slavish to me.

Nevertheless, my fourteen-year-old heart thumped and whacked as we read the romantic lines of the play, and when I got to the kissing place I leaned over and kissed Jo Ellen's warm though will-less mouth like a passionate grown-up lover. Her green eyes widened and she seemed a little amazed, but she did not respond or twitch or say anything, and as the silence deepened and I said, "Well," and she said, "Well," I got nervous myself, feeling I had slid into water way over my head. What if Jo Ellen spread the news at school or among the adults that I had taken it into my head to kiss her and left out the part about Shakespeare? And about its only being a play? I decided nothing would help except to get her to be committed and as far in over her head as I was, and the way to do that was to induce her to make an aggressive sexual move.

"Well," I said as firmly as I could manage in the breathy atmosphere, "now it is your turn to be Romeo, and I'll be Juliet." I laid out flat and stiff on my back in imitation of her and waited. This time the pause was as deep as a well and as wide as a barn door.

Then her voice came. "OK," and she raised up on one elbow to read by the gleam of the flashlight on the floor by my ear. We got to the vital part, and then she stopped. "Well, come on," I said, impatient with sudden social terror. "Romeo kisses Juliet. It's in the play." And to my intense relief she leaned over to kiss me. Then just before her lips arrived a massive earth-rattling, thundering-end-of-the-world banging began in one side of my head that drove me into an instant frenzy and sent me hollering and pounding my poor skull on the cement floor. Had lightning struck, or psychosomatic illness? No. Drawn by the flashlight, a simple-minded moth had bumbled into my ear and was thrashing its great wings against my eardrum. The result was similar to being in a load of cement inside a cement mixer.

Humiliation followed, Jo Ellen's mother having to be called to warm some oil and pour it into my ear canal to drown the idiot, and when everything settled back into place with the moth blissfully dead and washed away, Jo Ellen had retreated into a deep, complete, nervous silence.

I saw both her and Pamela a few more times, and something volcanic must have built up in our tense relationships. Both of them were under increasing pressure from their parents to voluntarily drop me as a friend, particularly as they were beginning to attend Rainbow Star dinners and Cotillion dances where their formal gowns billowed awkwardly around their skinny, undeveloped bodies, and the fact that the children of cooks and clerks were excluded was what gave the event half its meaning. Jo Ellen and Pamela were cultivating the closed, artificially smiling faces and tight nasal voices of women expected to direct servants. I was of the altogether wrong class to follow them along their narrow and difficult path. However winsome and appealing, my pirate Huck Finn ways could no longer be tolerated; soon I would be banished from Pamela's life. Never again would she say a word to me, even in the hallway at school, let alone be Tom Sawyer to my Huck Finn.

The last summer afternoon before my banishment from the kingdom of the Cotillion, we were all three together when something strange happened with the flitty Jo Ellen. Perhaps her thirteen-year-old mind just went berserk. That afternoon as I got to Jo Ellen's front door, Pamela met me. "Go upstairs," she ordered anxiously. "Jo Ellen is acting funny."

As I leaped up the stairs to the rescue, Jo Ellen charged out of her parents' bedroom holding a loaded derringer. Rushing down the first step and then steadying the blunt-nosed pistol with both hands, she aimed at the center of my astonished forehead just six inches away and pulled the trigger two or three times. Enraged when the derringer failed to fire, she continued down the steps aiming at Pamela, chasing her out of the house and across a field. The wispy and outwardly passive Jo Ellen had out-butched everyone and had gotten the plot all screwed up and was trying to murder Romeo, Juliet, everybody! We never mentioned the incident; it wasn't a terribly unusual occurrence, given the number of pistols, rifles, and unexploded bombs in any household in our little town. Well, goodnight, Jo Ellen; goodnight, Pamela and Huck and moonlit rides; goodnight! goodnight! Romeo and Juliet, goodnight!

CATHIE NELSON

A Flower for Judith

Judith: I remember her so well. It would be unthinkable to shorten her name to Judy. A lot of my childhood is a blur but my first love stands out like a full moon on a clear night. She was the epitome of all I felt I should be: slim, graceful, with big blue eyes and a head full of soft brown curls. I especially remember her slender hands. She had beautifully manicured nails which were always perfect ovals with very prominent "half-moons." I never understood the special significance of having white half-spheres at the finger end of one's nails, but it was clearly a valued mark of young womanhood which I lacked. I presented a sorry contrast to Judith's sophistication, if a six year old can be said to be sophisticated. I was a chubby child and my mountain-of-flesh mother had already informed me, sighing, that I would resemble her as I grew older rather than my tall, tinker-toy father. I was told to wear long sleeves and learn to emulate Kate Smith.

I was an asthmatic child and clumsy. "DON'T RUN!! Do you want me to take you to the hospital again?" What's more, I couldn't sing. "Just mouth the words, you'll throw everyone off key." Worst of all was that in the late 1940s, home permanents had just become a consumer item and I was my mother's guinea pig; so, in addition to my chubby awkwardness, I usually had a head full of steel wool hair which smelled of ammonia.

Judith is the first person in my life that I remember well. I'm not sure what she saw in me. Perhaps it was that I was smart and did well in school; it was considered ok to do well in school if you were a girl and were only six. Somehow we were friends. We shared secrets which I no longer remember, read books together and tried to manicure my nails so I would have half-moons like hers. It never worked.

One Saturday when we were in the third grade, we were to go to a school play together. I had saved my allowance and on that morning I walked downtown and bought her a flower, a gardenia. I brought it home in its white box, happy to think of surprising her. When I reached home, my mother asked me what was in the box.

"A flower for Judith," I said.

Her breath whistled as she sucked it in and drew away from me. She glared at me with eyes of steel as she turned to look for my father. I didn't understand but I was used to finding out about rules only after I had broken them. After a conference in the kitchen which I couldn't hear, they both drove me to Judith's. That seemed strange since my father usually chauffeured me around, but something told me not to ask questions. I went to give my flower to Judith while my parents talked to her mother. When we came outside, ready to go, the grown-ups gave me unfriendly, sideways looks. I was used to that with my mother but felt uneasy at the unanimity: what had I done? Judith and I went to the play, but when I got home my mother announced that I would not be allowed to play with her again, nor was I to speak to her at school. I was stunned and didn't understand. We spoke once, in whispers in the cloak room. Her mother had said the same thing. Out of confusion and embarrassment, we never spoke to each other again.

In the summer between the third and fourth grades we moved to a dusty little town in the southern part of the county where I spent the rest of my childhood. I knew I still wasn't the poised, beautiful daughter my mother wished for but I was still smart. My grades were good, I won essay contests and spelling bees. She could brag to her friends that I was brilliant. "Why, just listen to these grades!" my mother, who never went beyond the ninth grade, would say to the neighbors. Although I was not the cross between Rita Hayworth and Betty Crocker which she apparently wanted, she seemed willing to accept what I had to offer. It was an uneasy compromise.

At Christmas time of the year I was in the ninth grade, I could tell something special was going to happen. My mother was softer to me; she smiled more. Obviously the change from her usual disapproval had something to do with the coming holiday. I began to realize that I was going to get a present of special significance which would have something to do with growing up. I felt warmth with anticipation although I knew that a slide rule, which was my fondest desire, wouldn't make her smile with such pleasant mystery.

Christmas morning came; we unwrapped the usual socks and underwear. When everyone was finished, my mother smiled at me with tears in her eyes and said, "There's one more, very special present." She left the room and came back with a rectangular box. It felt very heavy when she put it into my hands. As she sat down to watch me, my father put his arm around her; they were both smiling. I unwrapped the present and opened the box. I didn't know what I was seeing.

"Take it out of the box!"

I lifted it out but was so unprepared that I couldn't recognize what I held, even when it was in full view. I must have looked very puzzled.

"It's an iron!!" she said, "For your hope chest!"

Tears were streaming down her face as she looked at me tenderly. I felt nothing except a vague, confused disappointment. An iron, WHY? Hope chest! I'm only fourteen! Why is she crying and looking so happy? I was aware that there was something I should understand, some message to be gleaned, but at the time it all seemed strange and inexplicable. Many years later I could understand that for my uneducated, ex-farmer mother, an iron was the proper preparation for female adulthood. When I was younger, my intelligence was something for her to brag about, but now that I was growing older it was time to get down to the real business of survival. I had to learn to catch a man.

Even though her iron message didn't get through consciously, my grades started to go down. It no longer mattered to anyone but me whether I took Trigonometry or Home Economics. Well, it did matter, but in a different way.

"TrigoNOMetry! Don't be ridiculous! With a personality like yours, you'd better learn to cook or you'll NEVER catch a man!"

She put the finishing touches on the death of my academic plans by announcing, two weeks before I was to start college, that I couldn't go. They needed to save the money for my brother's education.

"After all, he'll get married and have to take care of a wife and family and you'll have a husband to take care of you."

At that point, I really needed some understanding adult to encourage and support me but since that support and encouragement were not forthcoming, in the face of this additional obstacle, I gave in. I decided she was right. I was smart but my brains hadn't gotten me anywhere. Maybe the only way to take care of myself—my only choice in life—was to choose the proper man, the man who would give me a ". . . beautiful home, children, success! All that a woman could want!"

I married when I was nineteen. My husband's first gift to me was a big French cookbook. He wanted to be a dentist and to have a wife to give the dinner parties and to raise the children. If she was smart, that was ok, as long as she wasn't TOO smart. I worked, like a good wife, while he went to dental school. At night when he studied, I wasn't allowed to make noise.

In the spring just before he graduated from dental school, I became very sleepy. I had to quit work because I slept so much. A psychiatrist pointed out that my husband was about to reach his ultimate success—graduation from dental school. In contrast, I was far from my ultimate success, pregnancy. At the time I was relieved to know that there was a reason for the way I felt—just to give it a name made me feel less crazy. Now, twelve years later, I shake with rage at the idea that a full uterus equals success for a woman. My depression was my own righteous anger which I had turned in on myself. I was angry at my mother for not caring about my real talents, at my brother for taking my money so he could learn to design weapons, at my husband for stepping all over me to get what he wanted and expecting me to smile and say "Thank you!" Most of all, I was angry at myself for not fighting back and for not saying "NO!!" I understand all this now, at age thirty-five but at twenty-three I was simply relieved to know I wasn't crazy.

I loved the idea of having children. They came quickly, four in four years. Being a mother was hard work but wonderfully absorbing.

The children didn't care what I looked like or whether I was obnoxious about politics; they just accepted me and loved me for myself. That quality of total acceptance passes out of mother-child relationships fairly early, beginning when the child differentiates itself from the mother. As my fourth child grew older I decided I didn't want any more babies; I still wanted to be totally accepted and loved, but I needed to find a new source for love and acceptance. I chose myself as that source.

It was hard after all those years of seeking approval from

others to seek it instead from myself. Ironically, I decided to give up the approval of others just when I had a lot of it. I had achieved "success"—a handsome, successful husband, four beautiful children, a fancy house—all, as they say, that a woman could want. My life was defined by my relationships to others, however; I was what was missing.

At first, I resisted my friend's efforts to get me to join a consciousness-raising group. I knew without knowing that I would have to make profound changes in my life.

One week in C-R the topic announced for the next session was lesbianism. Everyone giggled but me. My insides turned to ice, my heart pounded and for the first time in twenty-two years Judith and the flower flashed into my mind. Somehow I managed to get out of the meeting without anyone noticing me. I sat behind the wheel of my car and shook. Many powerful feelings fought to reach the surface of my consciousness but I shoved them back. Was THAT what they all had thought when I gave that flower to Judith? But I was only seven or eight! Was that why my memories of her were so strong when they came up again? No! I just couldn't be a lesbian! I didn't WANT to be—it would be too hard! I don't remember the next meeting but I think I went and said something, anything to keep the others from seeing how I was affected and the turmoil I was in.

I was able to bury the issue of my feelings for other women under the problems I was encountering in my marriage and in going back to school. A few years later, however, as a good friend was leaving on vacation, I told her that I loved her. It seemed a natural thing at the time but it must have struck a chord in her because a week later, when she returned, she said she had to talk to me. When we were facing each other she said, "I know this sounds crazy but I think I've fallen in love with you."

Her words made me very happy and later, when she touched my hand, I knew I had never been touched like that by anyone. A feeling of wholeness came over me which has never left.

After the first few months of romantic discovery of each other, months which were wonderful in their lovingness and horrible in their frightening implications for the future, I began to face the idea of coming out. It seems hard to believe, but in the early part of our relationship we didn't use the term "lesbian" for the powerful feelings we were experiencing. A whole new world had opened up, a part of me with which I had never been in touch. I loved it—but I didn't feel like a lesbian. After the first giddiness had passed I began to try on the word lesbian: me? No! I would look funny in a crew cut. Certainly I could never learn to smoke cigars! My own stereotypes interfered with the unfolding of my new identity. Lesbians aren't mothers, I thought to myself; they probably don't like to cook or weave or do any of the things I like. Such were the fears and struggles which, for a long time, I either kept private or shared only with my lover.

Finally, I began to realize several things: that, for better or worse, I was/am a lesbian, that I wanted to leave my husband, and that I needed desperately to talk to other lesbians. I was too isolated to know any other lesbians at all. And I was so afraid of public exposure that I didn't want to ask around for someone to talk to. At the time, my lover didn't feel that she was a lesbian nor did she want any contact with other lesbians. The painful loneliness of that time has contributed to my decision to be as public a lesbian as I dare, given the threat of gay oppression and fear of a custody suit. I want to make myself available to support other women going through similar transitions and I can't do that from inside a closet.

Eventually I found my way to a therapy group composed of both gay and straight women. I made my way to the therapist's house on that first night feeling very anxious. What would I find inside? What would other lesbians be like? Would they accept me? Would I accept THEM? My knock was answered by a woman, slim and pretty, who looked like many other women. She introduced me to the other women in the group who were, again, very much like other women, only perhaps friendlier. My surprise at not finding a different species of human being blossomed into love for the women in my group, a growing acceptance of myself as a lesbian, and the courage to question, grow and change.

What about the woman I fell in love with? We're still in love with each other. Our relationship has survived both of our marriages; she is separated and my divorce is nearly final. We are working toward a future which includes living together with our children. Many of the issues which we are currently facing involve gay oppression. She is a shy person who feels intruded upon by my openness. I, in turn, feel oppressed and cut off from myself by her realistic fears of exposure. So far, we have survived many problems which were far thornier than the question of how open we are going to be; I have great confidence that we will face the issues ahead and resolve them in the non-coercive ways which are possible between people whose relationship is not based on one having power over the other.

Homophobia is also a factor in my relationships with my children. Before my oldest child will invite his friends over, he combs the house to make sure that all books with "lesbian" in the title are in my room and that the *"Lesbian Concentrate"* record is safely hidden behind *Tosca.* The other children seem less afraid of people outside the family knowing I am a lesbian, although they always remind me not to wear my "Support Gay Teachers and Schoolworkers" button to Open House at their school.

Coming out, a life-long process, involves conflict between my desire for complete openness and my respect for the privacy of the people whom I love most. I accept this conflict as part of my life, as I am growing to accept many parts of myself which I formerly rejected. When I think of my coming out, I think of the never-ending opening of the never-ending petals of a flower, that special, painful flower from so long ago.

MATILE POOR

A Loving Friendship

In the lesbian community, most of our talking and writing about love focuses on conventional love relationships in which women think of themselves as lovers or as a couple. But this is only one kind of loving, and there are other love relationships which we seldom talk about and explore. I want to tell the story of me and Corky, two women who have been friends for twenty-five years.

My loving friendship with Corky began in 1954 when we decided to be roommates at the University of Wisconsin. What may seem somewhat unusual about Corky's importance in my life is the fact that we have never lived in the same place since 1955, and usually we have lived thousands of miles apart. She lived in Boston; I lived in New York. I lived in Massachusetts; she lived in Africa. I lived in Europe; she lived in California. For the past fourteen years I have been in New Jersey and she has been in California. Still, our lives have been touched by one another, and I feel that she has been a part of major changes and decisions in my life.

In the past five years our lives have become more intertwined than before. I know that feminism and the women's movement helped us validate the meaningful friendship we already had. On an emotional level, however, what made our increasing closeness possible was that after twenty years of friendship we were finally able to openly express to one another the love we felt, and to accept it as a love which did not have the same expectations or boundaries as a conventional love relationship. With some sadness and even shame I look back and realize that I could not freely and openly express my love to Corky all those years, but when I did, it was a freeing and life-changing event for me.

I still remember a Friday night in the Fall of 1954 when Corky and I were talking in our room, and I turned around and looked at her on the bed, and I knew that I loved her and thought she was the most beautiful woman I had ever known. What Corky never knew until five years ago was that the "moment of realization" on that fall night has stayed with me all these years. In 1954, women did not talk openly about loving other women. I was especially afraid to tell her because at that time I was a lesbian drop-out. I had had relationships with women in high school, and I had tried to leave all that behind when I entered college. In high school, I had lived in such utter fear that my lesbianism would be found out that I decided in college I wanted to live without all that fear and conflict. I did not, therefore, want to have a conventional love relationship with Corky, or even to admit the strength of my feelings. Most of all, I did not want her to know about my past lesbian experiences, or to have any reason to think I was a lesbian. Corky knew nothing about lesbianism. In fact, she was probably the straightest person I knew as an adult. Even though I am still ashamed of my lack of courage to tell her all those years, she later said that she would have backed away if I had told her. For years, we had a beautiful and loving friendship, but along with it went a lot of denial about myself.

She married toward the end of college, and had three children. I married about five years later and had two children. I went to graduate school before having children; she went after having hers. She later separated from her husband, and I separated from mine. We seldom saw one another but on each visit we shared important parts of ourselves, and we wrote letters and talked on the phone. When Corky married, I remember thinking that we would never be close friends again. She always welcomed me whenever I could visit, though. It was certainly significant that within three weeks after I was married, I was back in Boston at her house. Having her in my life was always important to me. When she went to Libya to live for two years, she sent dozens of photos, and wrote wonderful letters which I still have. None of the events which I can recount explains the way I felt. I always had the sense that Corky was there whenever I needed her. When my husband asked me what I wanted for my fortieth birthday, I said that I wanted to go to San Francisco to visit Corky. Over the Christmas holidays in 1973 I saw her for the first time in about six years. During that visit we finally began to realize and to express how much we meant to one another. Our sharing was not something which happened in a day, or even a month, but over a period of months.

The conversation which began to break the barriers of twenty years began one Sunday morning in Glide Memorial Church in San Francisco. Corky and I were whispering to one another while the rock music played. She told me about the wonderful lesbians she had met in the women's studies program at San Francisco State, and how much she identified with these women. It was the first time in twenty years that either of us had said the word "lesbian" or talked about women loving women. I knew the time had come for us to acknowledge how special our friendship was and to be able to openly express love. I knew the time had come, but I did not know how to go ahead.

That afternoon when we went to Muir Woods, I was almost sick with anxiety. All that Corky and I never said began to unravel as we walked through the mist of the woods. We talked about our lives and the women we had become, and began to talk about the nature of a woman's love for other women. Corky reached for my hand and took it. We continued walking, holding on to one another. Later I wondered how it could have happened that we waited twenty years to clasp hands.

The conversations about love and about our friendship continued via letters and phone calls. We were both nervous and afraid. What did it all mean? What did we expect of one another after such a declaration? We knew that there was nothing conventional about our loving friendship, and yet, after twenty years, the subject of love was still difficult to deal with. This experience has made me think about the limitations we place on love, and how scared we are to openly experience it in other than conventional relationships. I realized how special we were to try to understand the depth of feelings of our friendship. After many conversations long distance, and letters, Corky telephoned me one April afternoon, and when I picked up the phone she said, "I love you, of course, I love you." We had finally reached a point where we could openly accept ourselves and each other.

I want to emphasize the importance of her response to me because this is the kind of acceptance of love which is sought in traditional love relationships but need not be restricted in that way. To have the feeling of her acceptance was a life-changing event for me, and I gained great sustenance, strength, and security from it. My marriage ended, other loves have come and gone, but I know that Corky is always there for me, as I am there for her. I also know that openly loving Corky freed me to openly love other women again. At the age of forty, I stopped being a lesbian dropout and re-entered. Corky also came out recently. There is no way to measure how much our friendship has changed our lives, or led us to where we are now. We have at last come to know ourselves, our vulnerable loving selves. Not only can we openly share our love for each other, and other women we love, but we can enjoy the intertwining of our lives in the lesbian community. We do not know enough about the loving friendship between women, stories as moving and beautiful as Lillian Hellman's *Julia*. How can we know the truth about women who have hidden it from themselves?

CORKY REPLIES:

Matile, old friend, a woman's movement binds us—fast feminists. When I said I know and love lesbians, you said, dear heart, it is I too. I too am a lesbian. I laugh to colors and concepts of woman love twenty years later, after lives of husbands and children. I say I have always loved you. You say you have always loved me. I hear music and smiles. Grow old and wise with me, we say.

JANE GURKO

Coming out in Berkeley, 1967

When I met Hastings, I was living alone, still licking my wounds two years after breaking up a longish, rottenish affair with Dan. Since Hastings was sensitive, my private life came out in a gush, all my fears about being too mental and unspontaneous, too alone.

Pretty soon, in the ordinary Berkeley way of things, we were making love. His guru-gear deserted him in bed, unfortunately, and after the most minimal of murmured praises and touches from me it was wham, bam, and "wow, you're some woman." I was left, as usual, shaking with physical frustration and nervous anxiety. My relations with men were classically lousy: I forgot about myself, tried to please them, did please them, and then felt resentful when my needs went unmet, but was too frightened to admit I had any that weren't identical to theirs. I fell for these pseudo-sensitive types, hoping I suppose that they would know what I wanted (which was more than I knew) and then give it to me. Hastings was no exception.

The day after we made love he told me he was married. I was shocked, but didn't know how to respond.

"It's all right," he said. "Sharon and I are trying to work out an open kind of thing. When I like another woman I really need to express my feelings physically. It doesn't threaten my commitment to her, and my life just isn't whole without it."

"How does she feel about it," I asked, taking my cue from him.

"Well, she's a lot younger. It hasn't been easy for her. But she's loosening up. We try to be honest with each other." He stroked his beard. "I'd really like you to meet her, I think you'd enjoy each other."

I was suddenly curious. Lured by this new plea, I forgot to be hurt or angry. A few days later, I met Sharon at their house. She looked at me with dark eyes full of interest. I took her hand and smiled back, relieved that the first moment was over, and very interested in turn by this girl who was apparently unhostile.

We quickly fell into easy talk. Hastings was happy and animated. This was definitely his element—people sharing and communicating, working out their feelings together. I saw him look tenderly at Sharon, and I remembered him telling me that he had once brought another woman into their menage and Sharon had exploded with jealous rage after two months. He was clearly testing the waters again, this time over me.

Sharon was rather quiet and secretive. She obviously preferred to listen and follow the energy of other people's talk.

As for me, I was in my element as much as Hass. I always got along well with couples, priding myself on the way I paid attention to wives and girlfriends. I was not one of those bitchy couple-breakers, spreading jealousy behind me like a bloody trail. I simply divided myself between the mates, and was thus attractive and safe to both. But of course, as a friend, I always went home alone.

This time, however, Hass and Sharon talked about my staying. They wanted to start a house, a community of six or eight people who would "really live together." Hass talked about shared work and weekly encounter meetings. I was dying for some kind of warm family life, but there had to be a solid couple as its nucleus.

By the following week we were reading real estate ads and happily discussing details. How would rooms be worked out, and money? We were excited, but still hedging around the main issue. Hastings was the one who got us down to business.

"Listen," he said, "if we're going to live together we have to get our sexual stuff out on the carpet."

Both scared, Sharon and I looked at each other: were we going to share Hass?

"I mean," he went on, "we have to draw the lines."

Sharon was stretched on the floor in what had been a casual pose. Without moving she had gone rigid. Acutely aware of my own fear as well as hers, I took a deep breath and said, "O.k. Now is certainly the time. What did you have in mind?"

"Well," he replied eagerly, "you know how I feel about monogamy. It's too limited, it just doesn't feel right to me. Sharon knows that I have a primary commitment to her, and that isn't affected by my sleeping with other women. I'm really attracted to you, Jane, making love to you seems right to me. If I can't have that freedom, I can't have marriage at all."

My stomach suddenly knotted, and I felt closed in. But Hass

was right, wasn't he? Freedom was good. People shouldn't try
to own each other. Families should be open and sharing. Everybody in Berkeley in 1967 knew that. Why did I feel a weight
on me? I couldn't respond to Hass, and looked toward Sharon
for help.

"Sharon?" I asked. She was stiff, but she looked up at me
with dark, imploring eyes. Then she said quietly, in a way
which must have hidden the struggle, "I know it's foolish, but
I'm just not that easy-going. I just can't . . . I've tried an affair
and couldn't . . . make a go of it."

The weight lifted and I breathed easier. On an impulse I
reached out my foot and gently prodded her on the behind. Oh,
how I sympathized with that tightness. I rocked her gently,
hoping to loosen her up. Sharon relaxed and accepted my touch.
We both forgot for the moment about Hastings and his freedom.

"I'm glad you tried that, honey," he broke in. "It takes courage
to overcome these old inhibitions. I had to struggle with jealousy
myself."

I felt Sharon begin to go tight again. Then, as I looked at the
girl beneath my feet, something about her posture struck me
with tangible force. I looked at her as if for the first time: her
rounded body, usually held rigid and aloof, was softened now
into its natural curves. With a pang I felt this body asking a
question, as the eyes had asked even from the first moment;
and I realized I had answered even then. I turned back to
Hastings with fresh interest.

"Of course I've been attracted to you from the start, Hass. But
I like Sharon, too. I want the freedom to be warm to her, like
now; in fact, I think your wife actually turns me on."

Hass beamed. "I think that's terrific. Women should be able
to express themselves physically with each other." He added,
"whatever you do is fine, as long as you don't exclude me."

Sharon gave me an odd smile, her eyes alight. She turned to
Hass and said, "How could we promise that? We've never been
there, we don't know what it feels like."

"There," he replied, "that's what I mean. If you're going to
go into a big romantic fantasy, forget it. They're exclusive by
definition. But physical affection, that's different."

Sharon and I must have looked as if someone had opened a
door, then shut it half way. The light from within still shone

on our faces, revealing mixed doubt and desire.

"But Hass," I put in, feeling my ground carefully, "Sharon's right. We have no experience with these feelings; if we express them, we can't promise where they'll take us. And I guess," I said, looking at Sharon, "we do have the feelings."

Sharon's eyes flashed back a dark look. We paused, waiting for Hass. He was becoming a little anxious now, but, unwilling to let his own desires go, took the lead again.

"Best thing to do to deflate adolescent romance," he said, "is to strip. Nothing so realistic as the naked body. Are you game?" He looked grimly from one to the other of us. Sharon seemed frankly scared, unwilling to expose herself to Hass. I was scared too, but not of him. What will she think of me? I wondered. I felt bony and awkward, suddenly envying Sharon's lovely fullness. With a sense of duty as grim as Hastings' I said, "Sure, I'm game."

Hass and I began to strip, very self-conscious and hearty about the whole thing. Sharon said, "I don't think I can," and slowly began to strip too. Hastings and I shuffled into the kitchen and began busily preparing food, sidling around each other, stealing quick glances, wondering what to do next.

Sharon hesitated in the living room. I saw the light go out, but still she didn't come. I was by now in a fever of desire, painfully conscious of my nudity, and fearing how Sharon might react to it. I knew without looking when she finally came in—I was electrified by her presence. She touched my flank as she passed and for a moment I forgot my body and its awkwardness. I recovered, hastily buttering bread, and waited for her to pass again. When she did, I turned to look. Hass had his back to us at the sink, and Sharon and I gazed at each other a long time. Yes, Sharon seemed to be saying silently, yes. I stared back, mesmerized. Naked, Sharon's body was even more enticingly muted than clothed. Her softness drew one in to her; she was silent and hidden, yet there was something magnetic about her, something so passionate that only silence could express it. The kitchen began to throb with three people's barely suppressed desires. Hastings apparently forgot that his demystification program wasn't exactly working, and after some forced small talk and token eating, he easily ushered us into the bedroom.

With the light out we all became self-conscious again.

Hastings was in the middle, and Sharon and I quickly began to stroke him. In a minute our hands met, grasped, explored each other—understood. We went back to Hass as if to some obstacle in our way that had to be patiently removed. We serviced him with all the double skill at our command, kneading, caressing, massaging, working out in technique what we withheld in emotion. After he came, Sharon and I touched each other in the dark. It was our turn now. Would he sleep? How would we manage? I felt our desire rising up in a single wave, and Hass, still dazed, must have felt our pressure unconsciously. He got up fretfully, and left the room.

We waited utterly still for a few seconds to be sure he was gone. Then we turned toward each other with a moan and embraced. At last, I thought. Stay out, Hass, stay out. Sharon said, "My God, you're beautiful," and a wave of passion unlike any I had ever known swept over me. I realized I had wanted her from the start—no, for years—and here she was, the forbidden, the longed-for, the dreamed-of woman, suddenly real and mine to hold. Was this what men felt, this sinking into softness, this open desire? I had focused myself so long on the man's needs in sex, I had never realized my own. Except in fantasy. Sharon said "Touch me," and I trembled. As we kissed I felt a power in myself that I had only dreamed of before, and soon I was lost in it, rocking and moaning, years of repressed desire pouring out of my limbs onto this unknown woman whose dream I had touched with my own. This must be the difference, I thought, for with men I could never know what they felt nor they me. And what they were was not what I wanted. *This* was it, this woman whose body was like my body, and who was asking me for herself. I stroked her breasts and they seemed a miracle to me—a woman's breasts for me to touch and kiss. Sharon seemed transported, and with a groan I reached down to feel the soft wet lips below. As my fingers closed over her clitoris Sharon cried out softly, and with a sharp pang my whole body began to throb. Sharon was gushing and when I thrust my fingers in I cried out myself, my pleasure rising up in me as Sharon, swelling toward climax, thrust back, once, twice, and came clutching me hard, shuddering in long violent shudders, and I, with my legs wrapped around her, burst in response. I held her through the spasms and then our slow floating down.

Sharon seemed dazed with pleasure. She said she had not been having orgasms with Hastings, and this had been so overwhelming, so unexpected. She looked at me with intense desire. The strain of staying quiet, of waiting for Hastings, began to tell on us. We both ached with the desire to have the night to ourselves. We looked at each other in wonder, and separated painfully when he finally came back in. Feigning sleep, we managed to avoid any real encounter, letting him climb into the middle without remark. Neither of us really slept that night, our presences fixed on each other, silently signalling over the bulky body between us. In the morning the light broke on the last act.

I awoke to find myself passionately in love, an entire new world opened to me. Sharon awoke to fear; in the light, the first thing we both saw was Hass. She could barely look at me, though I was sure her body remembered. Hastings himself woke vaguely uneasy. By the time we had dressed and eaten, a certainty had apparently formed in him. He marshalled us into the living room and sat down looking haggard, but firm.

"I can see what's happening," he said, "and it's just what I warned you about. You're really turned on to each other, which is o.k., but you're excluding me. I feel really threatened."

I suddenly felt threatened in turn. I had never anticipated being a rival to Hastings, but my whole sensual self had now to fight for its new life.

"But Hass," I countered, "we said we didn't know where it would go, and even now, if you don't let us play it out, we can't possibly grow beyond it, into the kind of thing you want."

"I realize that," said Hastings wearily, "but I'm telling you that I feel too threatened to let it go on. If you do go on, I'll walk out the door and not come back."

We both looked over at Sharon, who sat withdrawn and wary.

"Well?" said Hass.

Sharon turned a dark face on him. "What do you expect me to say?" she asked hostilely.

"I think you'll have to choose between us," I said gently, but my heart was beating wildly. What would I do in her place?

Sharon remained sunk into herself while we waited. She was clearly torn inside by the seemingly impossible conflict.

"I can't answer you now," she said finally. "I'll come see you tomorrow."

I left the house in a daze of pain and longing. Everything seemed unreal, the streets, the sun, my own apartment. She'd be a fool to leave him, I thought, I haven't got a chance. I didn't think about the reality of any relationship with her—no such thing existed yet. I didn't know her as a person at all, only as a trigger for this wild, obliterating passion. When she finally came I must have looked ravaged with anxiety. I went cold when I saw her armored, aloof bearing, and waited for the worst.

"Jane," she said in a cool voice, "I've decided to stay with my marriage. It's what I really want. I really love Hastings, and this hasn't changed my feelings for him." Her tone shifted slightly from cool to condescending. "I hope this hasn't hurt you in any way, or set you on a path . . . you know, made you . . ." She trailed off, delicately divorcing herself from the taint of my new destiny.

Her words hit me like a blow in the gut, and though I wanted to smash her cold control, it was a moment before I could say, "Well, you've probably made the right choice. And don't worry about me. Worry about Hass. He has a lot to learn, apparently." I tried hard to meet ice with ice as I showed her to the door.

She had the gall to phone me several times in the next two months, inviting me over while Hastings was away. "What he doesn't know won't hurt him," she said. Once I went, tied to a fantasy that was still the realest thing in my life.

Then I met a woman who fell in love with me and pursued me earnestly. I resisted at first, still tripping over the taboo. But I didn't resist for long. In one night I discovered the difference between passion and love, and banished Sharon from my dreams forever. But I thanked her in my heart before I shut the door; and Hastings too, who had ushered us unwittingly into our initiation. Until the ice was broken, I couldn't take the plunge.

JOAN NESTLE

An Old Story

I am now a liberated thirty-eight-year-old lesbian feminist but I wasn't always. In the late fifties and through the sixties, I was just a regular fem who spent long weekends in the back-room of the Sea Colony (a lesbian bar right off Abingdon Square in the Village), dancing close but sitting down when the red light came on because the cops were making one of their regular visits for a pay off. I dutifully lined up outside the bathroom to be handed my allotted length of toilet paper by the butch who spent the whole night alongside the skinny bathroom door dispensing paper and saying "only one at a time." But that is another story.

What I want to write about is an adventure I had one night. I lived at 417 East Ninth Street on the lower East Side of New York in a building that is, to this day, a lesbian heirloom. Some of the old railroad apartments with the bathroom in the hall and the bath tub in the kitchen have been passed from lesbian woman to lesbian woman for over fifteen years now. It was a Friday night and I was trying to get up the courage to go to the bar as I did every Friday night. I seldom went alone because I was scared. I wanted so much to be there but alone the experience was overwhelming. I finally decided to venture out. I wanted to meet someone. It was a late dark spring night. Since I was a fem, I had regular bar attire: a tight sweater to show off my breasts, and slacks that did not hide my (what I thought then) too wide hips. I had short hair and that caused problems. "I'm not their type," I would moan to friends when trying to explain why I couldn't meet the butch of my dreams.

Anyway this night I put a jacket over my costume because I had to walk the streets. For some reason, I never took the cross-town bus but always walked the long route across Second Avenue, down St. Marks Street and across Cooper Union Square, picked up 8th Street and continued until I reached my harbor on 8th Avenue.

When I walked the streets I was not a fem. If it was late and on the weekends and I was going looking, I thought of myself as a gay man cruising the streets. So I set off, hands stuffed in pockets, looking straight ahead, watching shadows, eager to get to the bar and yet knowing I would panic at the door. It must have been around 11:00; I was approaching Cooper Union. I don't remember the exact place but all of a sudden ahead of me in a dark side street I saw a man lurch and fall in the gutter. I changed my route and entered the strange street. He was lying in the middle of the road, a big heavy drunken man. I looked down at him. He is going to get run over if he stays here. And for the first time that night in between all the disguises and premeditated actions I was myself. I bent down and said, "You have to get on the sidewalk." He tried to move but couldn't lift himself. I am 5'2" and he seemed huge.

I felt a power flow into me—it was just the two of us alone on a night street both on the prowl and I could lift him. I put my hands under his shoulders and started yelling at him to help. His body lurched against mine; we both pulled, pushed, grunted, slipped and started all over again. I was covered in sweat, but I lifted him out of the gutter and dragged—walked him to the sidewalk. He thanked me as he slid along the wall. "Try to stay away from the gutter," I suggested, knowing he, like I, had a right to do what he wanted with his dark nights but death is not usually part of the game. I continued on my way rejoining 8th Street and for a few minutes I knew who I was. I was a strong woman who could use my body in strong ways; I was an adventurer defying a world that said I could love only in darkness; I was a woman who did unwomanly things and I was powerful. By the time I reached the Sea Colony, I was a fem again, frightened, looking for a strong woman to take care of me.

It has taken years for the strength to flow back, for the disguise to drop away, for me to understand what I was doing and who I have the right to be. It was a complicated world, the world of butch and fem, and I am only now beginning to understand it. I realize that in my writing of this I never gave a definition of "fem" but it is hard to look backward and sort out the concepts that stood behind the role that then seemed just myself. For me, to be a fem meant to be a woman with a body that other women wanted to touch; it meant worshipping the strength in other women's hands; it meant waiting to be seen, to be touched and then it meant giving. "Fem" didn't mean passivity; it meant a driving need and it meant performance. I wanted to be the best woman in bed for the woman who chose me. I wanted to be the reward for other women's strength. I created homes for strong women who lived in small uncared-for apartments and all the time I knew the power of my own hands but I kept them still.

Then, little by little, change came. I grew as the lesbian community grew. Separations of sex and mind, work and the weekends, political struggle for others and my own oppression started to break down; my fem mask shattered because it could not bear the weight of full living. There are too many stories to tell here. My fem years will always be a part of me, but I live in a new world now; and, while I cherish the courage of the past, I deeply celebrate the fullness of the present.

MARGARET SLOAN-HUNTER

Two Poems

I have not been fat all my life. One day it came to me how differently people have related to me as compared to twelve years ago when I was not fat. The poem was written as a response to the assumptions that people have about fat women, specifically fat Black women.

The Poet Speaks of Herself

It has come to my attention that possibly all big women
are misunderstood.
She has told me things
and hesitates on sharing them with you. Me she trusts . . .

There is a gentleness behind her
that you do not expect and therefore
you do not see.
Because she is a big and Black woman
you are fearful of her
as she enters your room.
I scoff at your image of strong, Black woman
for she has added each pound
in a wave of insecurity and weakness.
She cries almost daily
to rinse the pain from inside that enormous soul
but you are more at ease with her laughter
You lay at her chest for nurturance
so close you hardly see it slowly caving in
She no longer needs a place to be big;
they had that waiting for her at her birth bed.
What she needs, and what you can give her most,
is a place to be tiny.
She can grow from there.

I called my older sister Barbara one night to share my fear and pain over the discovery of fibroid tumors, which meant

possible surgery. That conversation led to a discussion of the
four generations of women on my mother's side of the family
who are all still living. We had what I call a "roots" discussion,
and I was filled with the legacy that each had knowingly or
unknowingly passed on to each other.

Connections to Generations
Through Life and Death

I lay on my back in my bed, and feel it
through my skin—this morbid swelling that
has invaded my body.
The tumor that has attached itself to my uterus.
I curse it, this imitation embryo that compels
my body to duplicate the events of my pregnancy of
ten years ago.
I hunger, thirst and tire more.
They want to pull out my womb.

I think of life . . .

I reflect on the four generations of Black females
in my family. All living.
My mother Virginia, 53, and her mother Emma who is 71;
my sister Barbara, 33, myself who is 29, and my child
Kathleen who is 9. All but Kathleen and me have no wombs.
All are Black. All are of me. All are me. I am them.

I think of death . . .

I remember my Aunt Johnnie who was strong and beautiful.
She was the sister of my grandmother born after
my mother. She was my mother's aunt, my great aunt.
Mother called her "baby auntie."
At twenty-one she moved up North from Chattanooga, a very
independent move for a single Black woman then.

She lived in Harlem. Down the street from Small's Paradise.
She worked at the Telephone Company. One of the few Black
    operators.
Whenever I acted up, my mother would say, in her most
    disapproving

tone, "You're just like Johnnie Mae."
I would walk away and smile as I turned into the next room.
As a child she played baseball. One day one of the children
got injured and Johnnie rode in the car to take him
to the "colored" hospital.
The car crashed. Johnnie was injured seriously on the leg.
A tumor—that deceased invader—lay dormant on her bone
until she was thirty-two years old.
The cancer spread throughout her body.
It ate her lungs away.
She died at age thirty-three. Two months before Billie Holliday.
In Harlem.
She never married. She never wanted to. She had no children.
My mother assured me, however, that she had
lots of boyfriends.
I was young, but I do remember her. She told me that I was
her favorite niece.
She was a Gemini also.
If Johnnie had lived, she would have been the first
that I'd told. I would have shared with her the most
intimate
parts of my life. She would have understood.
But the cancer . . . it grew . . . it spread.
It ate her insides away.
I think and I am scared to death . . .
I think of my womb . . . I think of my life.
For Emma who never dreamed . . .
For Virginia who dreamed of choices, but had no freedom to
    choose . . .
For Barbara who had the choice, but could not see it.
I choose.

They will not rip from me
this first home of my child.

BETH BRANT

Ride the Turtle's Back*

A woman grows hard and skinny.
She squeezes into small corners.
Her quick eyes uncover dust and cobwebs.
She reaches out
for flint and sparks fly in the air.
Flames turned loose on fields
burn down to bare seeds
we planted deep.

The corn is white and sweet.
Under its pale, perfect kernels
a rotting cob is betrayal.
It lies in our bloated stomachs.

I lie in grandmother's bed
and dream the earth into a turtle.
She carries us slowly across the universe.
The sun warms us.
At night the stars do tricks.
The moon caresses us.

We are listening for the sounds of food.

Mother's giving birth, Grandmother says.
Corn whispers.
The earth groans with labor
turning corn yellow in the sun.

I lie in Grandmother's bed.
We listen.

*Reprinted from *Mohawk Trail* (Ithaca: Firebrand Books, 1985).

IDA VSW RED

Naming

Last week I tried to introduce my lesbian lover, who is a teacher, to a colleague of mine, who is a librarian. Stumbling over the words, I jumbled their identities and embarrassed myself by introducing the librarian as "another member of Lesbian Schoolworkers" when what I meant was "another member of Women Library Workers." Of course! My lover is the Lesbian Schoolworker. The librarian followed her "glad to meet you" with a quick denial of the lesbian label. I blushingly mumbled an inadequate correction to the facts all of us already knew.

Introductions were painful to me long before I became woman-identified. Even though I was early versed in the correct order, format, titles, and gestures for the convention, my sensibilities have always balked at smooth performance of the familiar ritual. When I was young, I avoided introducing others, blocked the names of anyone I was introduced to, embarrassed my mother by my awkwardness, and felt dissatisfaction with the names, labels, descriptions, and identities hung on me by others.

First there is the matter of relationships—daughter, wife, mother, lover, friend, roommate, coworker. Sometimes I have wanted to claim these relationships for myself and those I introduce. More often I have chafed under the labeling and wished for less limiting, more imaginative introductions. In my small hometown I was first identified by relationship: as my mother's daughter. Two years ago I introduced *myself* as a daughter in a Mothertongue Readers' Theater script:

When I was a teenager, people said mother and I were like sisters, but actually I was always the daughter.

Did I continue to be a daughter when I became a wife? A mother? An independent agent? A lesbian?

What makes me a daughter? Blood, genes, love, care, or just the mothertapes that continue to repeat themselves endlessly in my thoughts?

Will I be a daughter all my life? Even when I reject the daughter role or am rejected by my mother? Even if she becomes childish? After her death?

I did not choose to be born a daughter—but what does being a daughter *mean*?

Perhaps simply that I have available to me a special life-long relationship with another woman, herself a daughter—a relationship not chosen, begun in dependence, charged with conflict, subject to change—but still available to me, one-half my responsibility for nurturing or neglecting.

Can daughtering mean something other than meeting or failing to meet my mother's expectations?

Can it be simply becoming the person I am—the person who exists only because I am my mother's daughter?

If relationship can come to mean being oneself to another, then I am content to call myself daughter—and mother. I still remember the shock of my first formal introduction as a mother. After the nursery school teacher introduced me as "Judith's mother," I began to wonder when I became a mother.

Was it the Christmas I was three, pushing my doll carriage 'round and 'round the house?

The night I removed my diaphragm too soon, allowing an egg to be fertilized?

The morning I felt kicks under my maternity smock?

The day my first child was born? The first moment I held her? When her suckling produced my milk?

When I planned my second child's conception? Did that deliberate choice make me more a mother?

Would I have been a mother if I had only conceived poems, only nurtured lovers, only "produced" myself?

Will I continue to be a mother all my life—even if I succeed in becoming a friend to my daughters?

"Friend" is the label my lover and I sometimes use for one

another even in liberated San Francisco in 1979. I prefer it to "roommate" but rank it below "the woman I live with" in non-committal honesty. I'd like to feel free to introduce her as "my lover," but this seldom seems appropriate outside lesbian circles. I take pride in avoiding the phrase when I think it would vulgarize our preciously intimate relationship, but I am saddened by the continuing necessity to avoid reference to lesbian love in order to protect one's job. I delight in being introduced by her as "my lover." Somehow "lover" seems more active than "wife." One becomes a lover by loving and being loved. One hardly becomes a wife by wifing and being wifed.

Even more loaded than the relationship hook is the professional or associational designation used in introductions. Certainly I want to be identified with the work I do in the world and others who share this work, but how often does the tag accurately describe the real work? Or the worker? No job title or professional association exists for the work I do: FACILITATING THE COMMUNICATION OF LIFE EXPERIENCES AND UNDERSTANDINGS AMONG PEOPLE. My education, my on-the-job training, my in-the-life experience, and my work coalesce in this communication process—a worthy profession. Only when one's work in the world is synonymous with one's life process will professional and associational labels become useful and desirable to me.

As I began to look at my work and life as process, the labels I had been assigned lost some of their authority and I began to feel competent to describe my changing self. I realized that naming might be considered a process rather than a fait accompli. In 1976 I examined the evolution of my names:

> Ida Virginia Sumner: The family myth is that at age two I gave my full name—even before asked—enthusing, "Ida-Dinna-Tunna-ha-ha-ha!" Already apologizing with a laugh for my delight in my existence? My grandmother called me "little sister" but seldom called her grandson "brother." Anyway, he was "BIG brother," like the government. When I insisted on simple clothes, my exasperated mother dubbed me "Plain Jane."

> Ida V. Sumner: A few close friends called me "Ida V" or "ivs," but usually I have been happily just "Ida," a name

that means happy and thirsty—but not at the same time. Thirsty for fame, I dreamed of romantic pseudonyms and stage names. College friends thought me affected to use the middle initial in my signature, so I didn't have the nerve when married to use *two* initials to preserve my whole past, as I wished to. I hated giving up my names to become "the former Miss Sumner," as the newspaper announcements read.

Mrs. John E. Wood: Married, I often forgot to use my husband's name. My mother, on the other hand, always remembered when addressing letters to me. My husband sometimes introduced me affectionately as his "child bride" or "little wife." His nephews called each of us "Johnnyida" because we were inextricably paired in their minds and I naturally signed my letters to his family with his name first, mine following. Sometimes it seems strange to me now to be called "Mommy" by my half-grown daughters.

Ida S. Wood: The moment the feminist press pointed out to me that surnames do not belong to women, I began to look forward to a name transplant. I thought I would reward myself with a pen name as soon as published. I got impatient and decided to change as soon as divorced. Finally, one day I found that my new name was there for the taking, so I took it.

Ida VSW Red: "Ida" for familiarity; "VSW" to preserve my history; and "Red" to herald my herstory.

Why "Red" for my woman name? Because red has always been my favorite color? Because it is simple, primary, strong? Because the single red geranium my grandmother grew was my favorite flower, vibrant life in a closed house? I was tending toward the choice for these uncomplicated reasons when I attended a conference of hospital librarians. It was a time of transition and decision in my life.

A therapist, whose recent dissertation on poetry therapy I admired, opened her session by coupling the participants, giving them ten minutes to get acquainted, then asking each one to introduce her partner with a poetic image. Judith, the therapist, introduced me this way:

I see Ida as a child's red rubber ball bouncing along a
winding country road. She bounces off the road,
through the woods toward fields of daisies, up a hill to
a fieldstone cottage. She bounces up the steps and
through an open door to a glowing fire on the hearth,
where she settles down to rest. As she looks around,
she discovers with delight that the floor-to-ceiling
bookcases are full. Slowly she realizes that the cottage
is her own and that she wrote all the books.

I was deeply affected by this introduction, cried with joy and
sadness. Joy that my childlike resiliency and vitality were still
visible. Sadness that I delayed so long in the early stages of this
search, this journey toward myself. The symbolism of the story
seems perfect. I followed the only road that society showed me
in the fifties—from my rural roots through school toward marriage. Still, my nonconformity let me bounce through the woods
of marriage and family my own way. Somehow, even the beautiful fieldstone wall and floor-to-ceiling bookcases my husband
built me failed to make our comfortable house into my permanent home. Again, my differences let me bounce into a field of
daisies on the other side. These represent the ideas and lifestyles
found in graduate school, new associations, and feminism. It
was an uphill journey from those discoveries to a place of my
own, filled with my own values, ideas, choices, and accomplish-
ments. I love both the comfort and peace by the fire's glow and
the assurance that the red rubber ball can be expected to roll
and bounce on to other discoveries and realizations. I hope the
products of my life will be available to other women.

After the conference, Judith suggested that I do something
good for myself on the weekend. I eagerly embraced this new
concept. I had been following a strenuous schedule of commuting, graduate school, family life, and working. After driving to
the Shenandoah National Park and spending the night in a
motel, I enjoyed a huge breakfast at a mountain lodge, wrote
and ruminated by the fireplace while the fog lifted, and walked
in the forest all day. I had never before given myself twenty-four
hours of pleasure and communion with myself. The first autum-
nal red was showing in the Virginia creepers. I was beginning
to have faith in this favorite season of mine that I could

reclaim my life, name myself, and live for myself.

To my amazement, my name change upset, confused, even angered some of my friends and relatives. My mother ripped sheets from a notepad listing her negative associations with "Red," including:

Red Skeleton   Red Eye
Red Buttons   Red Beard
Red Grange   Red Baron
Red Skelly   Red Blanket

Red Sox
Red Anarchist
Red Nosed Reindeer
Red Man
Red Communist

This is adding
red hot ashes
to our fire

My daughters, on the other hand, responded positively to the choice of "Red." One made me a coat of arms in her highschool art class. The other wrote me a touching poem that nostalgically lists some of the symbolic roles of red in our close relationship:

> . . . but thinking about Red.
> teaberries surprising the green ground,
> oxfords on the first day of school,
> gingham curtains framing my view,
> leaves rustling down past the blues,
> smile from a stranger-friend,
> pencil marks proclaiming an A,
> grosgrain ribbon wrapping a brown braid,
> cranberry strings draping a glitter-tree,
> geraniums by a back porch step,
> tulip among yellow daffs,
> paper hearts and doilies and paste,
> and Ida.

Judith D. Wood
© 1977

When I chose "Red," I kept it a secret, savored it in private for a long time. I liked the link to my red-headed mother, who was called "Red" or "Ruddy" when she was young. It was almost like having that nonexistent honor—a matriarchal surname. There is an old wives' tale that to a child anything sweet is good and anything red, pretty. I like to think my name connects my country child with my urban feminist.

Red seems more and more appropriate to me as I touch my long-unacknowledged anger. I thought I had little to say about anger until the consciousness-raising Mother-tongue script-writing process elicited a history from me which I called "Autobiography of a Madwoman." I am slowly accepting the legitimacy of my anger and looking for ways to use it productively in the world. I am willing at last to be known as an angry woman. Finally, I want to be known for seriousness of purpose—in my relationships, in my work, in my use of names, in my anger, and in the process of becoming the person I am.

While I try to introduce myself to you, I am distracted by a cacophony of internal voices bickering, interrupting with their versions of my story, defining me, contradicting my reality, unnaming me, revising my history, correcting my language, luring me away from my center, making me crazy.

Shut up, you voices! You media distortions, you male historians, you scratched mothertapes, you warped social mores, you liars!

I have listened to you long enough. I am trying to hear my own voice sometimes weak as a whisper, breaking with tears, stuttering with ambivalence and fear, hoarsening with anger.

Still, I am determined to introduce myself to you as a loving woman. Of course the damned voices continue their static:

"You a loving woman?" They scream with derisive laughter. "You, loving? You who leave your loving husband, grieve your loving mother, shock your loving friends, disappoint your loving teachers, separate from your loving children, reject the pain of loving? You?" They screech hysterically.

It is true. I love in strange ways. I used to love by trying to please, giving of myself, and losing myself to love. I succeeded.

When feminism seeped into the husk left in my place by love, I began trying to love myself. First I loved another woman.

The voices can easily upset my balance still, but pouring my love, energy, and attention into women—including myself—is becoming as natural to me as breathing, though still as radical as fire.

Feminist lesbianism seems to me an earth-shaking way of becoming a woman, loving.

It has given me the power to name myself. I want other women to name themselves to me so we can exchange experiences and understandings about our loving, anger, work, naming, and living processes. I value self-naming rituals, But I still don't care for introductions.

JEANNE CORDOVA

Trauma in the Heterosexual Zone

I was a late bloomer. I remembered being scandalized in the summer of my 17th year when a friend used the word "shit." I never heard the words "gay" or "non-Catholic" until I had become both. Until I was 22 it seemed I always found out about the important things—sex, bad words, alcohol, women, love— ipso facto, that is, after I had committed the fact.

Yes, I was a teen-age lesbian. But in honesty, I owe it all to my high school gym teacher, the Camp Fire Girls and the Convent.

It was an accident to begin with. My freshman year in high school I fell in love with my gym teacher. Unfortunately, she didn't return my adoration; actually, she didn't even notice it. She left me the following summer; actually, she got a better job somewhere else. Nevertheless, this was enough to throw me into a major depression for months. Coincidentally, I happened to be going steady, as they used to say, with the high school basketball star. When my gym teacher packed her volleyballs, baseballs and basketballs and split, I ripped Davie's little silver basketball pendant off my neck and threw it after her.

Anxious about my depression and confused by its source, my mother sent me to summer camp to get away from it all.

The cure was perfect. Two days after I arrived I fell in love with my counselor. She looked a lot like my high school gym teacher. Conveniently, I caught a quick, long-lasting cold and had to move my bunk into the tent where she slept. Conveniently, she had a bad back. Conveniently, we developed the ritual of nightly back rubs—hiking up and down the mountains can be very hard on the vertebrae.

One evening I was sitting on the edge of her cot sort of rubbing her back, sort of dozing off, feeling warm and happy. She turned her head and whispered, "I love you"; and my world fell apart and came back together in the most beautiful way. I never remember hearing those words before the summer of my 16th year and I've never heard them again in quite the same way.

Catastrophe struck again as my 18th year, a strong Catholic

background and lack of heterosexual drive led me into the convent. Yes, a young, untouched Sister Mary Sappho. Suffice it to say, the convent was hell. It was a giant, mothball closet where all us moths kept bumping into each other because there was nothing else to do.

The phone rang one Sunday evening in Conventland. It was Mabel, a lay friend of Mother Superior. My fellow Sisters were in the dining room watching *Peyton Place*. After a lengthy discussion about nothing (later I was to learn this sort of conversation is called "flirting"), Mabel decided to come over and meet me. Mabel walked through the front door . . . I looked at her and she looked at me and we decided not to watch *Peyton Place*. The next thing I knew I was sitting on the couch in her apartment, she was handing me a whiskey sour and I was babbling out my life story with particular emphasis on the part about my gym teacher and camp counselor.

Many hours later we pulled back into the convent parking lot; I was drunk. As I opened the car door and turned to say something poignant and romantic to her, I fell out of the car and landed on the pavement. The whole evening had been a series of arriving at new points without planning to get there. Ipso factos. Like the points at which I found myself lying on her living room floor, and the point at which I felt like I was floating on her ceiling.

I broke the vow of Obedience seven months before I was supposed to take it. I never understood what Chastity meant until the morning after. Poverty, however, I can still say seven years later, is my true calling. I can't say I really understood Mabel—she joined the convent the day I left it—I understood what we shared together.

When I was 23 and bought my first pair of prescription glasses, I remember being shocked at the clarity of the world. Trees and houses and letters on the freeway off-ramps did not really slide into each other in a confusing blur. So it was with what Mabel taught me. The confusion of the past 10 years fell together. With my new Mabelized glasses of adulthood I saw clearly the beginning of who I was and the end of trauma in the heterosexual zone.

Although I could see my way out of that zone, I had a great deal of trouble finding the lost continent of Lesbos. I wandered about the straight wastelands of California State University at Los Angeles for many months. I lived in one of those coed apartment buildings where every morning at 6 o'clock you'd look down the corridor and see all the boys tiptoing back to their own apartments.

One night in the middle of this wasteland, Paul tiptoed into my apartment and stayed for six months. Now I can honestly say I loved Paul, still do. However, that had nothing to do with why I decided to have an affair with him. I am very analytical and take pride in weighing all the factors before making important decisions. So I weighed Paul. And it was fine and he was fine, but when his father died and he left for San Francisco, I failed to go into depressive withdrawal symptoms as is the case with me and lost love.

I decided to be more aggressive in my search for true sapphic love. In order to believe in the wholesome sincerity of my next move, one must understand that my naivete at the time was so acute as to approach insanity. I was 19. I grew up in a Chapel. I had never lived in a big city. I had never seen a dirty movie. I didn't know there was a war going on. I thought I was Chicano and blacks and whites were as good as me. I thought "Student Radicalism and Demonstrations" was a new sociology class. I didn't know what I was doing. I placed an ad in the *Free Press*—classified.

YOUNG, LONELY
GAY WOMAN
Would like to meet similar
woman for friendship. Please
call.

I thought the "for friendship" part was very sophisticated. Reading other obviously well-thought-out ads convinced me it was important to say exactly what I meant. I had hoped to meet a woman who would tell me about being a lesbian in "the gay life."

Thirty-seven men and two women called. One person stood out—Toni. Her voice sounded warm and pleasant so I invited her over.

My straight roommate and I were having coffee when her knock

came. I rushed to answer the door. There stood my 5'9",
bleached-blond, two-inch-fingernailed, 39-year-old, rouge-
painted happy hooker. I stepped out before she could step in.
I didn't know how I was going to explain my new "friend" to
my roommate. I was too shocked to explain her to myself.

I remember sitting on the couch in a friend's empty apartment
as Toni kept saying, "You're so young . . . your voice sounded
older on the phone . . . damn, you're young!" After 10 minutes
of this repetitious conversation, it seemed dialogue between us
had reached an impasse. We couldn't find much in common.
Toni left. Two days later a florist came to deliver a single yellow
rose. The card read: "Be careful, baby." That was the last I ever
heard from Toni.

I felt older. That short episode opened my eyes to the adult
world. I decided to be more discriminating.

Standing in the Cal. State registration line four months later,
I had every good intention. But the woman in the next line kept
staring at me. At first I discounted her. People often looked at
me strangely when I went out in public with my jeans and
motorcycle jacket. I have long since learned that most of us
have some sort of magnificent obsession with classifying people
according to gender. One of the fundamental dynamics of the
universal subconscious seems to be the ability to decide, "Is it
a boy or a girl?" I can now see that my dress style might have
presented room for doubt. Often, I think homophobia (heterosexual fear of homosexuals) is nothing more or less than the
straight person's anger at being so confused.

But Bobbi wasn't looking at me that way. I got the distinct
impression she knew and liked what she was looking at. I
realized I was being cruised by a woman! I was uncomfortable
with her confident public openness. I sighed with relief as her
turn came before mine and she turned to leave. A half-hour
later I walked out of the registration building by myself. On a
bench by the front door sat Bobbi. I remember she had a very
friendly smile, and I remember her big green Cadillac as we
zipped down the freeway toward her apartment.

Bobbi was not a biology major but she knew a great deal about
the human body. I, in psychology, knew about people and feelings. One might say we embarked on a crash Information Exchange Program. The course came to a rather abbreviated end

when it became clear that both of us were hopelessly addicted to our own specialties.

Sometimes I think Bobbi was important to my life because she taught me a few basics which were not without practical value in my future. At the time, however, meeting Bobbi only further discouraged me.

I declared both straight and gay life emotionally null and void. I decided to fall in love with my career. For six months my *Introduction to Psychology* text and I carried on a meaningful but unromantic relationship. I decided to make one last effort.

It was spring and baseball season. All during my childhood and adolescence, I had played softball on the women's ball teams. All during my childhood and adolescence, my mother tried to make me stop. All during my childhood and adolescence, I insisted that I loved to play softball, and, besides, my friends were on the teams and I wanted to be with them.

Now in my sophomore year in college I was getting smart. Suddenly I knew why my mother wasn't entranced with my athletic prowess! I threw my psychology book out of bed and called the Department of Parks and Recreation. This time I knew what I was doing. I joined the local women's AA city softball team.

I dressed very carefully for my first day of practice. I went to Thrifty's and bought a pair of heavy, white, athletic socks and a new mitt. I took them home and rolled both in the dirt to make them look worn and professional. Then I washed the socks and saddle-soaped my mitt. Next I dragged out my old rubber-cleated softball shoes; I didn't have to roll them in the dirt. They were so professional they almost fell apart when I put them on. I selected my oldest pair of jeans and donned my Cal. State sweat shirt. The latter was my credibility symbol. I topped off my wardrobe with a ragged green Pendleton that Mabel had forgotten to take with her. I was ready.

My offense lasted about five minutes after I got there. I knew that "I had arrived!" because all the other women were dressed exactly as I was. The problem was they knew what they were doing and I was still a rookie. As I leaned over the drinking faucet next to third base, the catcher came over and asked, "Are you gay?"

I choked on my carbon dioxide. As I looked up to see who was being questioned, my worst fears were confirmed. "I . . . what . . . well, you see, I like to think I have the capacity for both joy and sadness." Academia won out.

I was alone again at the drinking faucet. I was sure the catcher would tell the others, "Forget it. She's just a young uptight smart-ass." My heart fell to my rubber cleats as I turned to take my lonely position at third. Suddenly a short fly destined for shallow left field sailed over my head. I ran back, the left fielder ran forward. I saw her glove and mine reach for the ball, and then I felt her body crash into mine. The ball fell to the ground seconds after we did, but I didn't see it. I was looking into the twinkling blue eyes of the left fielder! She had the warmest smile. For me, the game was over. I wanted to find that catcher and shout. "Yes! Yes I'm gay! What do you think I'm doing here?!"

MARGARET CRUIKSHANK

A Slice of My Life

The first woman I had a lesbian relationship with called herself Tiny Hero, or TH for short. Her mother, whose name was Gertrude, she called Fordie Ann. TH called me many things, including Kitty Kitzmueller, which she sometimes shortened to Kit. She gave my breasts good Polish names—Sophie and Stella.

TH wanted very badly to get a WASP name by marriage. For a time she dated an ex-seminarian with a WASP name and not much else to recommend him. When he broke off their engagement, she was very hurt. I comforted her. Out of that drawing closer a lesbian relationship developed. But long before we caught on to what was happening between us, we invited a third woman to move into TH's apartment at the same time I did. Like us, she was the product of a small Catholic women's college. TH called her by her full name, Marcia Ann Scholastica Ness, Scholastica having been added when Marcia converted to Catholicism. During the baptismal ceremony, a candle carried by one of her friends set fire to her veil—a small incident which delighted the pagan heart of TH and foreshadowed Marcia Ann's later involvements with Rome.

Beginning a lesbian alliance with a roommate in a very small apartment, occupied by a third woman, had its special intricacies and awkwardnesses, among them the bedroom arrangement: the three single beds had no room between them and no room between walls and beds except in front. It would have been an ideal bedroom to display to a suspicious parent. Before Tiny Hero and I knew we wanted to sleep together, we had chosen the outer beds. I can still see us, two rather slight, dark-haired women separated by a very large blond Norwegian.

One night at 3 A.M. we awoke to the sounds of choking. M.A.S. Ness was clutching at the rosary she wore around her neck, which had become tangled up in the scapular she also wore around her neck. TH and I cut them loose, perhaps saving her life. Cradle Catholics who were by then lapsed Catholics, we judged Marcia Ann's religious zeal with the bored detachment of regular Sunday visitors to the zoo who know the chimp will be scratching his crotch. We protested angrily, though, when Marcia Ann's spiritual advisor, one Father Brendan, announced that he would thenceforth interpret the will of God for her. Sometime later she decided to go to Vietnam to see for herself if the U.S. ought to be involved. (I was never sure if Father Brendan and Mother Church could be blamed for this third threat to her life, but my opinion of the priest was not improved when I ran into him several years later in Minnesota. The woman I loved was with me. Brendan looked at her and asked, "Is this your son?")

Tiny Hero, on the other hand, was sometimes mistaken for my sister, an error we encouraged because of course it gave us a good cover.

TH had a fine sense of humor—playful, fanciful, irreverent. I was irreverent myself but the quality was not so fundamental to me and was more intellectual than emotional. But mockery came very naturally to her, and she was later to sum up the feminist movement in a single word—"whining." I loved the funny stories TH wove around Chicago politicians, people we knew, people in her past like Regina Coeli, or wholly made-up people, for example, stories of the midget we would capture to do our housework—our "midge." What rich material TH would pluck from the Jimmy Carter saga, I thought in the fall of 1976. And from his relatives. But I could only guess, because in 1972, TH stopped all communication with me. She later got married. Perhaps she meant to blot out her lesbian past.

Many of the women who were with us in a Catholic graduate school had passed through parochial schools. We each had our little collection of bizarre tales, of pagan babies ransomed, for example, and spectacular apparitions of the Blessed Virgin. But Tiny Hero could take stories from other women's troves and embellish them. I used to let her tell about an imposing nun in my past, a professor and Reverend Mother named Aloysius Steinbrenner, whose experiences of convent intrigue must have sharpened her understanding of English political history. Since Bloody Mary was a Catholic, Aloysius Steinbrenner could not of course accept her nickname. We were told to consider her tactless, not bloody. The younger sister of Aloysius Steinbrenner, Eunice Steinbrenner, was nearly as formidable as

Aloysius herself, especially when she expounded her two favorite subjects: the delights of virginity and the importance of the
Dead Sea Scrolls.

The uniformly repellent school songs of Catholic women's
colleges especially delighted Tiny Hero, and whenever she
met a woman fresh from St. Mary of the Woods or Incarnate
Word or Mater Dolorosa, she asked to hear her school song.
TH amused herself with these lines from the school song of
St. Prachna's, the college attended by M.A.S. Ness and earlier
by me:

> When in faith and knowledge grounded
> Enter we the world of strife
> May thy counsels, strong and holy,
> Aid us in our course through life.

Since the nuns had a vested interest in promoting virginity,
we were shaped for a world of strife in which the next best
thing to no sex at all is very little, with the accompanying
and conflicting message that a woman should have many
babies. The existence of male-female relationships in this future world was grudgingly admitted, while the only relationship that would be meaningful to many of us was never even
mentioned. Much of the knowledge in which we were
grounded, however, was nearly as useless to straights as it
was to young lesbians. All that TH recalled of her college
ethics class, for example (besides the sexist doctrine that the
life of the fetus is more important than the life of the mother),
is the lesson that if you are on a bulldozer fleeing from your
enemy, and come to a bridge only as wide as the bulldozer,
and see a baby lying in the middle of the bridge, you may
morally continue driving even though the baby is certain to
be killed. You have chosen only to avoid being killed by your
enemy, you have not directly chosen to flatten the infant.

How one applied such cases to the complexities of life was
not clear—attraction to other women, for example—but luck-
ily, neither TH nor I felt any guilt about our relationship, at
least after the initial uncertainties. Why I was spared guilt I
do not know, but other Catholic lesbians who were also spared
agree that we told ourselves something like this: loving her
feels so good it can't be wicked; or: if I am doing this it cannot

be wrong. Perhaps mentors like Aloysius Steinbrenner and Father Brendan had only a temporary hold on our minds; perhaps we were learning, in our early and mid-twenties, to accept some Catholic ideas, on social justice for example, but to root out of our lives any Catholic notions about sex.

But it was easier to reject the strong and holy counsel to live ignorant of our bodies than to achieve a healthy self-knowledge and self-acceptance. These days when I think of Tiny Hero I wonder how it was possible to live happily for three years with a woman I loved, who loved me, and not once discuss lesbianism. We sometimes alluded to and laughed at the disapproval we knew we would get if our families or friends understood that we loved each other. But that was all. Like so many other young women in the 1960s and earlier, we must have thought that we couldn't be lesbians because lesbians were hateful creatures— we just happened to love each other. We chose a person who just happened to be a woman. A ludicrous self-deception that now seems, but it was a convenient, guilt-free attitude. We could sleep together without needing to reassure ourselves that we were normal. Of course we were normal. This attitude had one overwhelming disadvantage, though: it discouraged us from seeing our love relationship as a wholly serious commitment to grow and develop together. Instead it was a pre-marriage idyll. Neither of us dated much or felt any desire to be married. But not being able to imagine a creative alternative to marriage, even though we were living one, we unconsciously ascribed an inferior status to our love, our non-marriage. We ourselves mirrored the prejudice of a society unwilling to respect a union of women, of lesbians.

The "second wave" of feminism in the 1970s helped many of us who were developing into lesbians to understand ourselves, to be more open about our feelings, and to acknowledge that we were, in fact, lesbians. But in the sixties I rarely talked about emotions or even thought much about them. When I look back on my three years with TH, I am struck by our nearly totally unreflective attitude toward relationships in general or our own emotional life. Since we got along smoothly and liked each other's company enough to spend many hours of each day together, we surely had chances to notice things about ourselves, if we had been noticing anything about emotional responses in those days. The extraordinary pleasure of a companionship and intimacy which did not depend on a man must have bound us. We were secure in our love and wholly devoted to each other, but we were emotionally undernourished. Presumably doctoral students in literature knew something second-hand about emotional life—we valued writers who described it best—but the vital connection to our own psyches was missing.

Our jock needs we met admirably, TH having stolen a football which we tossed around in the park where we also played tennis and swam. We were great Cubs fans and felt oppressed if our teaching schedules conflicted with Ladies Day (and sometimes canceled class when they did). But looking back I suspect that the great harmony and serenity of our relationship came not so much from compatibility (though in part it did) but from the superficiality of our emotions. Or from our inability to bring our deeper feelings to the surface. In those years I taught Arnold's poem "The Buried Life" with great enthusiasm, not suspecting that a part of my own life was buried. Tiny Hero and I could not tell each other what we needed; we could not even tell ourselves.

I think we were drawn together by a need to be mothered and an even greater need to escape from domineering fathers. Those needs we met well, but the unhealthy emotional climates of our families had given us highly developed defenses and the habit of suppression. When we did get angry, our explosions were not clarifying. Our convent schooling made us comfortable with abstractions, detached, and ignorant of the complexities of emotional life; it reinforced the fear of sex and of intimacy which afflicted our families, Italian/Polish in her case, German/Irish in mine.

These are the sorts of recollections one likes to test against the recollections of the other person involved. I badly miss the chance to do that with TH. I wonder if she thinks of her three years with me and how she thinks of that part of her life, if she is happy with a man, if she will ever love another woman, and what she thinks of her whole history as a woman.

Suspecting that three extremely happy years of my twenties were made possible by my emotional underdevelopment is rather painful. On the other hand, when I consider that all of the influences of my early life conditioned me to be bookish, one-sidedly bookish, I can rejoice at the emotional life I finally awoke to, through the young woman Father Brendan mistook for my son, a life which I might have missed entirely or merely gotten some faint impressions of. Even now, when I'm around academic women who seem untouched by deep feeling or who display the bleak, tight-lipped humor often found among unmarried women, I become uneasy. Like the person who survives an accident which kills her friends, I feel randomly selected to be only scarred by the strictures which can kill.

MONIKA KEHOE

The One That Got Away

I had been through it all at St. Anne's Academy. As a senior
in the parochial girls' high school, I had already been the object
of several crushes which I enjoyed immensely, and I had participated in numerous single-sex slumber parties, complete with
bathtub gin and canned gramophone jazz. One freshman ad-
mirer had knitted a sweater for me. Another had sent me flowers,
while a third had made a box of fudge which, as I dimly recall,
was so gooey and tasteless that I fed it to the dog, who munched
on it reluctantly.

Of course my mother must have found these all-night parties
and extravagant expressions of devotion from my classmates
rather strange but, since there was little communication between
us, and she had long ago given up trying to understand, much
less control me, she said nothing beyond some innocuous comment about the sweater being "pretty." I guessed that she might
have deluded herself into thinking a boy had sent the flowers
and given me the candy, but that was a fairly far-fetched idea
since she knew I seldom saw boys.

Fortunately, my mother was entirely unsophisticated in such
matters as are now referred to rather obliquely as "affectional
preference," and I wasn't about to enlighten her. She had had
an unrewarding life. Having been brought up in the country,
with English as a second language, she had dropped out of
school in the third grade. Married early and long unable to have
a child, she was already past middle-age when I was born. After
that achievement, my father promptly left her. She and I not
only didn't speak the same language, we lived in different centuries as well as in different worlds.

As a result of my previous amorous encounters, most of which
had blossomed in the locker room of the local YWCA swimming
pool, I was not too surprised to find that the women's college
I finally attended offered even more opportuntities for intimate
same-sex relationships to develop. I was surprised, however,
when the nun who was head of the French department began
showing more than strictly academic interest in my substandard

French pronunciation. To be singled out for such special notice by an instructor was naturally flattering and I even exerted some effort to improve my French phonemes just to please Sr. Eloise. In spite of the fact that French had been my mother tongue, my version apparently was not the acceptable Parisian dialect taught in college. Indeed, to my chagrin, Sr. Eloise labeled it "patois." *Cardenal* became my Bible. I had the text under my arm wherever I went. I really tried to learn to roll my r's and purse my lips in the approved manner. But my French prof seemed to think I needed more help so that she arranged to give me private lessons three times a week after classes were over for the day, and sometimes she set up a meeting on Saturday, as well.

Sr. Eloise was petite, with a typically Francophone lilt to her speech and flashing Gallic eyes which soon had me fantasizing in my other classes, where I was not so popular with the instructors, who began to accuse me of always daydreaming. They didn't know, of course, that "*la plume de ma tante*" and other equally important French phrases were ringing in my head.

My mentor and I met for our after-class language sessions, not in the college lecture hall, or even in her office, but in one of the music practice rooms in the convent which was on the far side of the campus. These rooms were small and narrow, originally designed as nuns' cells, with a window at one end and a door at the other containing a smoked glass panel which opened onto a wide corridor. Such a room was just big enough to hold a piano, the inevitable bench or stool, and one chair. The decor was rather dreary. All the walls were painted prison grey and relieved only by a large polychrome print of the bleeding Sacred Heart. Fortunately, the place was usually deserted in the late afternoon since the students preferred to arrange their practice schedules in the morning. It crossed my mind that it was almost as safe a setting for hanky-panky as were the locker rooms at the Y, which were always empty in the late afternoons as everybody made a quick getaway at the end of the swim period. I wondered, too, now and then, what the other nuns would think if they knew. Knew what? Nothing had really happened yet. Sr. Eloise was the epitome of propriety. Once when she was trying to shape my lips to emit the correct diphthong, I took her fingers and kissed the tips as she drew them hurriedly away.

But Sr. Eloise was not entirely impersonal. Often after tea-time, she brought me snacks from the refectory tucked up the ample sleeves of her habit—a piece of cake wrapped in a paper napkin, some cheese and crackers, or a bunch of grapes. I was too thin, she said, and she thought that hunger was causing the headaches I complained about now and then, partly to get her sympathy. Sometimes she would even massage the back of my neck with her tiny hands. This was a great excuse for me to put my head in her lap, close my eyes, and imagine she would soon bend over to kiss me, presumably on the back of the head. I didn't dare take the initiative. I was sure if I did, she'd get up, pick up her skirts, flounce out the door with her beads clicking, and leave me—maybe even dump me on the floor in the process. I didn't want to look ridiculous and my seat on the piano bench was precarious at best.

One day, with great bravado, I put my arms around her waist, as we got ready to leave, and lifted her up, just for fun. "Put me down," she said in a horrified whisper while I laughed rather lamely. Then I backed her against the wall, pressing my body against hers, pretending I would not let her go. She reached for the beads that hung at her side and distracted me completely by starting to say the Hail Mary in a soft voice. Programmed as I was, I responded with the last part of the ancient prayer as I stepped back somewhat shamefacedly to break the erotic spell. That was our last after-class French lesson.

All of this was admittedly pretty frustrating for me but, since nothing ever really happened between us, I didn't mention any of my "impure thoughts" in Confession. Anyway, I usually had enough other stuff to tell about activities with friends who were far less inhibited than Sr. Eloise.

Confession was, nevertheless, always something of an ordeal. If any of us "weirdos," as we had been persuaded to think of ourselves, albeit indulgently, went to the young priest who was assistant pastor in our parish, we got the third degree. Once, I remember, I was refused absolution, and that bothered me a bit until the next Saturday when I went back to old Father O'Brien for Confession. He was deaf and usually hollered his questions for anybody in the church to hear, but he never said anything too incriminating because he seldom knew what the penitent had said anyway. The penance he gave was guaranteed to be the same each time—"Say three Hail Marys"—and he could be counted on to give absolution to a murderer. Most of the congregation avoided him but he was a blessing for anyone in my predicament.

Now as I look back on this hectic period of my youth, I marvel at the little conflict that I had as a result of defying the basic tenets of my faith. I never felt guilty. I never felt sorry and I never worried about eternal damnation or any of the other purportedly disagreeable consequences of my amoral behavior. I enjoyed myself thoroughly. It was all a rather delightful game which I am sometimes tempted to play today, half a century later.

PAT PARKER

Goat Child

I. 1944-1956

"you were a mistake"
my mother told me
ever since i've been
trying to make up.
couldn't really imagine
her/him in bed &
me coming 4 yrs after
the last sister
& to make things worse
i come blasting in
2 months too soon.
maybe the war did it
& to top the whole thing off
i'm the fourth girl
& was my father pissed.
caught pneumonia &
got hung up in incubator
for three months
finally made it out,
but the bed was too big
so my sister lost her doll bed.
another enemy quickly made.
& my old man being typical
spade businessman
too much credit—too little capital
loses his shop, &
we move to what is now
suburbs of Houston only
it had weeds and space
move to our own home
away from two-story brick
project where i found my
cousin's condom & blew it up

& good-bye cousins to
one room—tin roof playhouse
with tarzan making beams,
tin #2 washtub, maggot-filled
outhouse and super rats/
but i did try to please then.
football, baseball, fishing,
best yard cutter on the block.
two guns hanging from my hips
in the best Texas tradition
& me bad pistol pete holding
up all visitors for nickels
& wiping out roaches faster
than the durango kid ever could.
but even the best cowboys need learning
so they herded me back to school
but i remembered nursery school
& nurses with long needles
hell no i won't go,
but i went & had to leave
my guns/ could only take
my boots & the teacher
300 lbs. of don'ts
& i cried thru a whole day
of turtles, lizards, pretty
pictures, crayons, & glue.
came back all ready to
hang up the second day
but the teacher showed
us her paddle—heavy
wood, hand fitted paddle
with holes drilled to
suck the flesh/ no tears
so i settled down &
fought my way thru first grade
defending my right to
wear cowboy boots even if
i was a girl which no one
had bothered to tell me
about at home/ swung

into 2nd grade right into
economics/ 50¢ notebook
which mother couldn't
buy that day & i couldn't
tell the teacher that rap
so i copped one from the
doctor's son who could
afford it easy, but he
had numbered his pages
& i couldn't explain why
my book began on pg. 9
& the teacher calls
my sister who had been
her star #1 pupil
four years ago who
immediately denies that
her mother had bought it
& there i was a caught
thief at seven years old.
conditions improved/
looked like i was going
to make it till 5th grade
& i got beat all day
for stealing a 15¢ pack
of paper which i didn't,
but couldn't say because the
girl that did was too big
& the teacher got religion
& bought me steak sandwiches
from then on & even put me
in the glee club which was
indeed a most generous act.
& 6th grade was worse cause
oldest sister #2 had been
there & the teacher had
a good memory for bad ones.
& it wasn't until
i recited the night
before christmas
three times on our

class program that
she forgave me

II.

the goat left this child
me still trying to butt
my way in or out
& i came home dripping
blood & panic rode in
on my shoulders.
her slipped to the store
returned clutching a
box of kotex in a sack
twice as large.
"now you can have babies,
so keep your panties up"
& i couldn't see the
connection between me &
babies cause i wasn't
even thinking of marriage
& that always came first.
& him having to admit that
i really was a girl &
all of a sudden no more
football, not even touch
or anything & now getting
angry because i still
didn't like dolls &
all this time me not knowing
that the real hang up
was something called virginity
which i had already lost
2 years ago to a really
hard up rapist that i
never could tell my parents
about, not really knowing what
had happened but somehow
feeling it would not be
to my advantage.

twelve years old
& in southern baptists
tradition that meant
the leaving of childhood
& the latest acceptable
time to go to God
so with pleas of the
family image ringing
in my ears/ i went
baptism/ no evil spirit
left/ just cold & wet
waiting to be struck
down for fraud
& now mickey—a
baptism present to
replace delmonte
who replaced scotty
who replaced queen
who went mad and
ran thru the streets
foaming with me
climbing fences to
cut her off at the pass
but mickey a pup
already at my knees
orange, blue tongued
chow who ate on his
trainer who played with
his food and him brings
the victor to me/
scared but even more
afraid of it being
known & mickey just
as afraid as me, but
we learned and i
unchained him &
took the christmas
bike and rode free
miles and miles
& mickey running

ahead challenging
any one or dog to
get too close.
the goat came charging back
& my sisters could no
longer tell me
& the fights won in the day
lost when him came
at night, but renewed
each day with each new welt
& the boys at school
learned that him was crazy
& off to the jr. prom
with the faggot in the
church choir/ the only
acceptable male other
than him & the hate
chickens, ducks &
rabbits who ate their
young when I forgot
to put in more salt and
beatings and the volleyball
team i almost made varsity
but the gym floor & stitches
& better grades to apologize
pajama parties & mothers
who knew to go to bed
dirty jokes that i
didn't quite understand
& beer and drunkenness
the friend who always
imitated me clomping
the cha cha & never
saw my pain/ horns
shrank until senior
year & debate champion
who really wanted to
write but more afraid
of the coach who
knew i was the next

great spade lawyer
& failed the only
boy i ever loved to
make sure i didn't
get married/ her
pissed because i didn't get the
scholarships/ the big one
me who never told of
the little one that
would have kept me
in texas/ new pastures
for the goat.

OUT

run to California
& golden streets
& big money
& freedom to go
anywhere & not being
served in new mexico
or arizona/ not stopping
to record that &
california streets
reeked of past glories
and wine and blood
and this brave young
goat blasting full
steam into everything
breaking the landlady's
window while showing
a young delinquent
a backhand & running
like hell; laughing
till it hurt &
his ole lady was
paying me to keep him out
of trouble
college and the german
who didn't want me

to know his language
& decided maybe adolph
wasn't so great after
all.
journalism
a friend who
cut her forearms
to commit suicide
& me offering to help
her do it right
& retired lady colonel
who didn't think i
liked her class &
this young beast
emphatically affirmed
her/ journalism "C"
a little dark buddha
walked in with folder
"i'd like to see more
of your writing"/ me
awed——a man—who
knew about the goat.

III. 1962-1966

"I am a man,"
the buddha said—
come with me &
i will show you
the ways of woman.
come with me &
i will show you
the world of being—
the world of pain
the world of joy
the world of hate
the world of love
come walk with me
i will show you
why&—you are.

this goat-child charged
muscles tensed,
leaped, trampled
into a new time
a time of talk
a time of wine
parties & me
not knowing the words,
the gestures,
not knowing
history or heritage,
not knowing
the liars or their lies,
but sensing, somewhere
my head—hooded
allowed to breathe,
but not to see—
a blind goat charging
"I am a man,
the buddha said,
come with me &
i will show you
the ways of woman."
this goat saw & felt
the blood run,
leave my body—
i could not find the eyes,
no heart, no limbs
only blood, deep dark
blood that was life
that was dead—
scraped away
with a surgeon's knife.
scrapped into regret
scrapped into pain
non-existent,
but real, real!
and the herds
herds of goats
herds of sheep

& the shepherds—
give me your milk
give me your wool
& we will feed you
we will protect you
the shepherds came
& taught me skills
to provide for them.
"come with me &
i will show you
the ways of woman"
& i learned
i learned hate
i learned jealousy
i learned my skills—
to cook—to fuck
to wash—to fuck
to iron—to fuck
to clean—to fuck
to care—to fuck
to wait—fuck
this goat-child cried
& screamed & ran
& the buddha's smile left
& his wisdom faded
& his throne crumbled
& the buddha left &
returned a shepherd.
in that leaving
the goat-child died—
the goat-child died
& a woman was born.

NANCY E. KRODY

On Being A Lesbian Christian

Though I've known since I was seven that I was somehow different from my friends and classmates, it was nearly thirty years before I was able to come to terms with my lesbianism fully. Through public schools in and near Cincinnati, six years at Ohio State University (1956-62), and two years at a seminary, I was definitely a "closet case." I had frequent emotional crushes on straight girl/woman friends, but was unable to seek out lesbians because I had no idea how or where to find them. During college I lived with my grandparents, so I was spared the pain of a dormitory situation where the dating pressures of the late 1950's would have been unbearable. I was not under strong family pressure to date or marry, although my mother reported that her high school home economics students were horrified to hear that her twenty-one-year-old daughter wasn't yet married: "She's an old maid."

During those school years, I had only occasional glimmers of interest in males, none of which involved sexual fantasizing, and nothing that could be called a "date" till my seminary years. At that point, I was close to a fellow seminarian, a gay man who helped me face up to being a lesbian. At one point we toyed with the idea of a "convenience marriage," but realized such a union would be a travesty on marriage, and dropped the idea.

I decided to go to seminary out of what seemed to me to be a genuine "call" to the ministry and a particular interest in the campus ministry, but I ran into a brick wall with my first-choice school. The required autobiographical statement raised a red (lavender?) flag for the admissions committee—one simply didn't admit to never having dated—and they urged me to consult an elderly woman psychologist on the Ohio State faculty. That proved to be a most uncomfortable experience for both of us. The school then rejected me, suggesting that I limit myself to laywork in a local church somewhere. My bitterness at their decision led me to apply simultaneously for admission to the Peace Corps (then in the first flush of its glamor for college students) and to Crozer Seminary, which had sent a recruiter to our campus. A telegram inviting my participation in a Peace Corps project in Central America arrived the same week as word of acceptance from Crozer, which at the time put more faith in academic ability than in psychological testing for its incoming students. After several days of wrestling with the decision, I packed for seminary.

I was the only woman in the three-year Bachelor of Divinity program during my two years at Crozer. During the first year, I received an award for the highest grades. In general I felt well accepted by the students and faculty as a serious woman with gifts for the ministry. My contacts with the wives of faculty and students were infrequent and usually strained. I worked many non-class hours in the library, so came to know area alumni and older students well. My field work took me into a Congregational (United Church of Christ) Church and an American Baptist Church in the area. During April of my second year (Holy Week to be exact), my seminary "career" came to an abrupt halt, dashing my dream of becoming an ordained minister. Looking toward its approaching centennial, Crozer had established a faculty-student committee to discuss how to enhance "community" at the school. As representative of the single, dormitory students on the committee, I voiced my concern at one meeting about the gay men on campus who had to find their community in the bars in Chester rather than within the presumably-Christian seminary community. However, before I could more specifically name people, I had to say that I was also a homosexual. Never was there a more naive coming-out or more swift retribution!

I was quickly moved out of the dorm, where I was the only woman, into an empty apartment (normally reserved for married students)—apparently out of fear that I would contaminate the men in the dorm. God knows what the faculty's conception of lesbianism was! I was allowed to finish my courses in the next few weeks, then had to leave campus. Eventually I found a job and I was permitted to return for one course per semester during what would have been my senior year, at the end of which I watched my gay brothers graduate and get ordained. They of course had *not* come out. I had been seeing a psychiatrist before this happened, but the seminary officials decided that I had not become sufficiently "normal" by the end of the third year to be recommended for ordination. Hence, I was told not to reapply for admission to complete my degree. I think my transcript carries some such euphemism as "medical problems." Two faculty members did not agree with the decision, but were powerless to change it. At least they provided some moral support and friendship, which was about all I had to help me retain any sense of self-respect. Many years later, both expressed their chagrin at what happened and their guilt at having done nothing to change it.

What did I learn from this agonizing experience? Most of all, I now knew what power the knowledge of my lesbianism put into the hands of people who control others' lives—clergy, educators, police, money-controllers, etc. I learned the hard way what I knew instinctively, but chose to ignore: keep quiet! My theoretical ideas about pastoral care and Christian concern were thrown into turmoil. There was no open, supportive women's or gay liberation movement in the early 1960's, and liberation theology was many years in the future. I felt in my guts that I was right and that my reading of the Christian message allowed a place for me in this world, but I didn't know how to convince others of it or even how to find another lesbian. I occasionally saw a semi-pornographic novel written by a straight man getting his kicks, but my fantasies were nothing like those described in such "lesbian" novels. And I found no comfort in the many indexes of books that I searched in hope of a friendly word about my "condition," for all the professional experts called me sick or criminal or sinful. My head and heart said otherwise, but in society's eyes I was no "expert."

It was many years before I learned that other lesbians existed and was able to find the literature written by the real experts— those of us who are lesbians. I learned what gay pride was all about from Byrna Aronson, the first lesbian I knew, who I met through a mutual friend. My mentor was very involved in the early attempts at building a gay movement in Pennsylvania and in seeking civil rights legislation. Byrna had learned what she knew from Barbara Gittings, one of the earliest open lesbians in the contemporary gay movement and the person most responsible for getting good literature by and about gays into libraries in the United States. She has also helped form many caucuses within professional associations. In recent years other women and men have been kicked out of seminaries from coast to coast—or denied admission in the first place—with some of them fighting back and some moving on to more hospitable institutions. Today there is greatly increased support for such people, as more and more students and teachers in religious schools speak out on our behalf. But there's a long way to go.

Since 1974 I have been more outspoken locally and nationally as a lesbian Christian—one of the few women to do so without fear of losing her job. I am assistant editor of the *Journal of Ecumenical Studies*, published at Temple University in Philadelphia. Both Temple and my union have protective clauses in their contracts. My colleagues know I am a lesbian and have invited me to lecture to their classes on gay liberation and religion. In 1974, I preached my "coming out" sermon in my local parish, a United Church of Christ congregation, and received strong support from my pastor and most church members.

Also, I have paid my dues in the women-in-religion movement through various ecumenical projects and have earned a right to be heard by my denomination through many years of service—as an elder in my local parish, as a member of social justice committees in my region, and as a member of national boards concerned with women's rights and the mission of the church. In addition, I have been a national leader of the United Church of Christ Gay Caucus, formed several months before the 1973 General Synod meeting at which the U.C.C. first supported gay rights. Of course there has been opposition to the work of the Caucus, but in many ways we have been accepted as part of the church.

Watching many of my sisters abandon the church in disgust because of its patriarchal, anti-woman, anti-gay stance, I must necessarily explain to them—and to myself—why I remain in an institution at whose hands I have suffered so much. I ache as much as anyone else at each new anti-gay proclamation from the church, from Anita Bryant's misguided fulminations to statements which hypocritically seem to support gay rights but at the same time say that homosexuals should not be ordained. How can I come to terms with an institution that has so badly used me and my sisters and brothers? I stay in—though with almost daily searching of that decision—primarily for three reasons.

First, the church is the "home" in which I was nurtured, where I learned what love and justice and liberation are about, where I learned what affirmation and dignity and wholeness mean. I have learned through the church that my sexuality is God-given and is good and necessary for me to be a full human being. As a Christian I am freed from the legalism of the old "thou shalt not" morality and bound instead to love God and neighbor as myself. I've learned, most importantly, to love myself. And thanks to the insights and experiences of the women's and gay liberation movements, I am able now to avoid the schizophrenic, closeted existence which far too many lesbians and gay men endure all their lives. I have seen the United Church of Christ take courageous positions about human sexuality issues despite strong opposition within our ranks, and I have seen people change as they give prayerful consideration to such issues. I have heard an older woman leader in the church say, "I've never met anyone of your kind before, but I've discovered from knowing you that you're just like everyone else!" People *do* change.

Second, the church is one of the most powerful institutions in American society. Its moral support is largely responsible for the oppressive laws that gay civil rights legislation seeks to change. If the church as a whole is ever to change its position on homosexuality, it will be because it learns to listen to the gay/lesbian clergy and lay persons who are within it and learns to know them as real persons. I have seen again and again that when you discover that someone you love and respect is gay it is impossible to reject that person totally, though many of us have feared telling our closest associates and our families. There are horror stories to be sure, and tragic suicides and "disownings," but more and more people are finding support in unexpected places when they dare to be open.

Third, I will not be heard if I leave the church. Only if I remain inside will my words have any effect on those who disagree. Only as they see my life as a responsible person who glories in her lesbianism and celebrates her covenant with her spouse will they come to understand and eventually to accept same-sex love. We have to legislate changed behavior, the sooner the better. But I would also like to see changed attitudes, and that takes time and effort and caring. Though my ministry is not recognized by ordination or paid position, I *have* a ministry as a bridge person between the lesbian/gay community on one hand and the religious community on the other. Though at times both sides may throw darts, a few of us must be there to talk the language of both sides, so that one day, God willing—and I think she will be—we can forget the labels and just *be*, with full acceptance for all lifestyles lived out in integrity. This includes the difficult task of ministering to the homophobic persons among us, in and out of the church: both the closed-minded heterosexuals and the closeted, fearful homosexuals.

May we all know liberation from our fears and pain and learn to love and affirm one another in our differences.

SUSAN MADDEN

On Keeping Ourselves Down

The best thing to come out of my chemical freedom will be a return of my power. My drug use (liquor) developed just at the time I was also beginning to explore my lesbian sexuality. And for twenty years now I've been using alcohol to keep myself down.

It's not so much that I've oppressed myself with alcohol. It's more as if I've undercut myself. Imagine yourself trying to stand tall and strong and someone (thing) is always nudging the back of your knees, threatening to down you with a clip. That's the image I have when I think of the way I've used liquor against myself.

For years now, ever since high school in fact, I've had people urge me to be more powerful. It's been expressed in different ways, depending on the speaker's own value system: "Susan, you're the most intelligent person I know whom I never hear say an intelligent thing"; "Susan, you don't remember any-thing"; "Susan, why didn't you say something then?" A couple of years ago, my friends were calling me YoYo, drawing atten-tion to my absentmindedness and not-quite-thereness. I liked the nickname.

People were trying to tell me something was out of step with the strong image I promise and the weak reality I deliver. I, too, felt some inner conflict, some way that I knew I had more strength, more focus, more direction, more power than I ever let out. It was as if I was holding back—sometimes I thought intentionally—but for what?

I've known I've had a "problem with alcohol" for years. I've described myself as a steady drinker (I drank every day), a heavy drinker (I drank a good deal every day), but I always took pride in being a controlled drinker (I rarely became very drunk). But somehow I've failed to see how damaging liquor has been to me.

It has contributed to making a ten-year relationship unsalvage-able. My lover and I were both drunks, she more obviously the drunk, me the enabler and subtle drunk, and by the time we began to look critically at the trouble our relationship was in, it was in such deep trouble I could not find the energy or the commitment to work to save it.

My drinking has been a constant source of worry to my current lover who, though recognizing the degree of control I have been able to exercise, still wisely feared a time when that control would crumble.

And drinking has allowed me to amble through my adult years, preventing me from coming to grips with my life and what I want out of it.

I've made it sound as if I've suffered consciously from the effects of alcohol all these years. Not so. Addictions always do something for the addict that she needs. So for the most part I've warmly embraced liquor. It's been a constant companion, a sure source of security. It's given me a predictable sensation of well-being and a comfortable feeling of safety. The book *Love and Addiction* describes what makes an addiction thus:

> Addiction takes place with an experience sufficiently safe, predictable, and repetitive to serve as a bulwark for a person's consciousness, allowing (her) an ever-present opportunity for escape and reassurance.[1]

That's what liquor has been for me, a means of escape into a reassuring world of easy camaraderie where, as I see it, everyone is friendly and no one has the drive to do anything difficult. That's the world liquor has enabled me to create for myself.

Other lesbians have created other worlds for themselves through chemicals. Nike Soberdyke, who writes in the New York lesbian separatist newsjournal *Tribad*, created an illusion of strength and competence for herself:

> I never quarreled with myself over any part of my drinking. I consciously accepted my alcohol intake as necessary for survival. After all, the patriarchy was out there actively killing women and in order to absorb all this, plus maintain the strength to fight back, I had to numb the nerves, calm the sensibilities. I rationalized this drinking around the theme of avoid burnout, be politically effective.[2]

Susan's world and Nike's world are different because they satisfy different illusions—one seeks respite from thought, the other respite from struggle—but they are identical in their ultimate purpose, to surround both addicts with a drug-induced sense of security, to provide both addicts with a respite from their feelings. There is an eerie calm, a muting of experience with chemical dependency. Addicts are not quite there. They have a buffer between themselves and life.

A note from my journal:

> I do like the part of how alcohol allows one to space out, to waft away, to be a little apart from what's going on. Always being sober sounds stark and bleak to me.

I believe that as a woman I have learned well several techniques that we all are taught to use in keeping ourselves down. To be really effective I enlisted the help of an addiction in doing this. Anything might have done: Alcohol, street drugs, prescription drugs, nicotine, television, sex, work, being in "love." I chose alcohol. The important point is to use this drug/person/activity as a way of blotting out what your life could be about. Here's how I describe the techniques of powerlessness that our culture teaches women:

1. *Be muzzy-headed.* Maintain a constant state of semi-confusion and vagueness. Don't think clearly about what's going on in your life and be very careful not to think clearly about what *you* want. Don't listen when people tell you things.

2. *Be secretive.* Don't let your friends or others know intimate things about yourself, your wants, thoughts, feelings, fears. Stay in the closet. Above all, don't let your most intimate person know what you want. Keep quiet.

3. *Be a martyr.* Always put the other person first. Protect them from reality. Be unconditionally nurturing and supportive.

4. *Be pleasant.* Smile. Most women have already developed this into a rote response, smiling regardless of the content of what is transpiring. This is good. Also, if you can't say something nice, don't say anything at all.

5. *Develop a dependable addiction.* This will allow you to successfully maintain the other four behaviors.

So far, these techniques are familiar to any woman. They are not only techniques for keeping ourselves down, they are the norms prescribed for each of us if we want to be our society's definition of feminine.

But I have found that I as a lesbian have a special relationship to these strictures, a unique vulnerability that traps me on my knees. To be whole and strong I need to share what is most important about myself, my identity as a lesbian, my commitment to love women. Once I have said this, to myself and important others, I can go on to build a life I respect, a world I cherish. But my society will not tolerate this identity, hates me for my love, wishes to destroy what I would build. The admonition to Be Secretive is a matter of survival for me and all lesbians where it is a wise suggestion for other women.

In our society we are prone to addictive behavior because of this contradiction: assertiveness is valued in words but is in fact suppressed. We are told how good it is to be special, independent, creative, different from others, but our society in fact rewards conformity and punishes deviance. In this process, individuals, especially those who *are* different in some significant way, are smothered. They turn to addictions for solace.

As a lesbian I find that exercising constraint and experiencing subjugation are as much a part of my daily life as moving my body and breathing. I turned to addictions to help me keep my secret. And by adopting an addiction, by keeping my secret, I developed the ways to keep myself down—a pleasant demeanor, a martyr's stance, and a foggy brain.

What addiction accomplishes for us lesbians is to cut us off, to protect us, from some feelings we need to recognize, share, and exorcise. The most dangerous feeling to bury is *self-hate*. There is probably no exaggerating the depths of our self disgust. Not only do we have to bear the burden of self-hate borne in this woman-hating culture by all women. Superimposed on this is the fact of our having been told directly or indirectly how abominable we are since the first moment of our sexuality/identity/life style choice. We all must assess how deep the resulting psychic scars really are. We drink so as to mask self-loathing. I drank so as not to kill myself, yet.

And we drink to drown out fear and rage. Our addiction protects us from experiencing the totality and the severity of our oppression. To look clearly at our society's attitudes toward us is to invite paralyzing fear. To reflect clearly on the interests served by these attitudes is to open ourselves to a consuming rage. I drank so as not to kill, yet.

But in numbing myself out to the bad feelings, I block myself too from the good ones. By being afraid to experience my self-hate, my fear and my rage, I prevent myself from experiencing my own liberation. We cannot fully feel the joy in being ourselves and the pride in being lesbian if we are absorbed in not feeling. I drank and was thus unable to love.

I believe we have the potential for making ourselves free. We can be free of self-hate by admitting its existence, examining its roots, and living beyond its confines. We can be free of fear by recognizing what is fantasy and what is reality in our fear, by sharing it with our sisters, and by building trust in each other. We can be free of rage by letting it out where we feel safe and eventually letting some of it out where it belongs. We can learn to live freely within ourselves, among ourselves, and— perhaps some day—within society.

We can do none of these things when we're fully absorbed by our addictions. I want freedom and power for myself, and to achieve them I must give up alcohol. I want freedom and power for you, my sisters, and to achieve them I want you to give up whatever is keeping you down.

Notes

1. Stanton Peele, Love and Addiction, New York: New American Library, 1975, p., 177.

2. Nike Soberdyke, "Death $3.49 a Gallon—Alcoholism and the Lesbian Community," Tribad, May-June, 1978, p. 2.

MAREE MARTIN

Fifteen Years Ago

In Rockaway Beach, New York, not long after I came out (in the summer of 1964 when I was twenty), I spent a typical Friday night hanging out at the bungalow of my last male lover, Dick. With us were my first woman lover, Roz; my friend Lana, who was spending the weekend, and a woman I didn't know named Pam, who was Dick's friend. In those days, if you had money, you usually did the "Village" scene: Washington Square, the Park, the bars. But if you were broke, you partied at someone's place. This was one of the no-money nights.

We popped "reds" (barbiturates) and drank a lot of coffee. Pam was obviously very attracted to Lana, who looked like a lesbian in her short-cropped platinum blond hair, black horn-rimmed glasses, men's bermuda shorts, tailored shirt and flashy pinky ring—all obvious signs in those days. Lana was not interested, and she went to bed.

Later I had to take Pam home in Dick's car. At an intersection we rammed into another car when the brakes didn't work. Nobody was hurt but we were in trouble because I didn't have my license with me, and Dick had no registration papers for the car. When the cop came, I noticed that he looked intently at me, reading my "butch" appearance. He quizzed Pam and learned that she had been at our party all night. When he asked her age and she said fifteen I was scared. A minor!

At headquarters we were turned over to squad detectives and carted off to different rooms to be questioned. I was asked how long I knew Pam, what we were doing all night, did I have boyfriends. I was confused because I didn't know why I was being held. Later the cops arrested Lana and Dick (hiding behind his front door); and when Roz came to the police station to help us, she was arrested, too, after admitting that she'd been at the party.

Soon we understood: using the threat of the youth house or reform school or worse, the police had coerced Pam (a known delinquent minor) into telling the story *their way*, and signing a sworn statement that we three lesbians detained her at Dick's apartment all night, where we fed her "reds" and made sexual advances. We were being charged with "impairing the morals of a minor." There were no charges mentioned having anything to do with an auto accident or an improperly registered vehicle.

Outraged that we were actually going to jail, the three of us were taken to Manhattan South to be processed. In the holding cell were about ten other women—prostitutes, shoplifters, and a woman who had been arrested for hitting a cop. I thought their real crime was surviving. We were put into a paddy wagon and taken back out to Queens to the 103rd precinct for the night. We were placed in separate cells, five by eight feet, with foot-thick walls between them. We could talk but we couldn't see each other. The bed was a wooden slab smoothed by many coats of jail-green paint. All three walls had a stenciled warning: DEFACING THESE WALLS IS A MISDEMEANOR AND IS PUNISHABLE BY LAW.

When we asked the matron if we could have some paper and pencils so we could "play," she brought us jail stationery and pencils. We tore the paper into small squares and began writing each other notes. We were able to stand on our beds on the right sides of our cells and reach up over the fine mesh (placed there so inmates can't touch each other) and pass our notes back and forth. On little pieces of two by three inch papers we managed to cram enough erotica to fill a small notebook.

By the time we got bored with our note writing, the matron had cut off our paper supply, and Roz had fallen asleep. Then Lana and I (who were having a small affair at the time, although I was going with Roz), decided it would be a challenge to "get it on" in different cells without waking Roz, or being heard by the matron one door away. We climbed above the fine mesh and reached out our arms and hands so that we could actually touch each other. That took some dexterity. We had a hard time not falling, not making noise, and especially not laughing. If anyone had been listening to us it would have sounded as if someone were directing traffic in a whisper. "To the right a little . . . over this way . . . up a little . . . to the right . . . right, dummy, right . . . O.K., there, there, that's it . . ."

Unfortunately we were interrupted by the loud clanking of keys. Roz half awake muttered "Who is it?" and in came a drunken woman in her fifties whose shins were still bleeding from the cops' attack on her. She screamed and cursed all night long.

The next morning the men who arrested us took us to Kew Gardens, where we were all together in a large cell. We talked about how cold we had been the night before. We admitted our fears. But we laughed when we remembered what had happened when the guard had told us to strip to the skin. Nobody wanted to be first, and we all stalled. Then when we were naked we felt indignant when the guard ordered us to "bend over and spread 'em."

As we were led into the courtroom we silently nudged each other as we glanced around and spotted my mother and Roz's parents. We also saw Dick on the side opposite us where the male prisoners are brought in. He was handcuffed and looked shabby and terrible. I guess we did too. I remember being *really* scared for the first time when the bailiff called our individual names vs. the State of New York on section whatever it was of the penal code, a vice charge. I could hear a rather noisy court go silent for this juicy case.

The charges were read. Those of us who had records had our past offenses read. The judge decided to release Roz to her parents' custody without setting bail because she had no record. Lana was released. Because he was over 21 and rented the apartment where the party was held, and because he had a past record, Dick was held on $500 bond. And, *only* because I'd been arrested before, never convicted, I was also held on $500 bond. I was shocked because it never occurred to me that I would be held. I was beginning to wonder if they could make their absurd charge stick.

I was taken back to my cell to await the bus from the Department of Corrections to deliver me to the Women's House of Detention, a rat-infested condemned building in Greenwich Village. It was a good two hours before I was led out of the building and onto this cage on wheels, and it was just backing out when someone called, "Hold it! Hold that bus." I found out that my mother and Lana, who had absolutely no money, had spent two hours pleading with a bail bondsman to spring me. He finally accepted Lana's two rings, one onyx and heavy gold and the other jade and gold, both worth about $500 . . . the price of my freedom.

Ten weeks later we had to appear for trial. Dick sat in jail the whole time, as I would have without those rings. I thought we didn't have a chance because the young lawyer appointed to represent us spoke to us for only a few minutes, not long enough to find out what really went on the night of the party. He didn't seem very concerned as he advised us not to testify, to let him do the talking.

When the charge was read, "impairing the morals of a minor," I could see Roz's parents shrinking in their seats and I could see fear on her face. The police testified first, using words like "lesbians . . . molest . . . pushing dope . . ." They were supposedly protecting Pam but instead they were using her, making her tell lies designed to "fix those lezzies," as I imagined them saying to themselves. We had no witnesses and I thought our case was lost.

Then Pam's mother was put on the stand, and our lawyer got her to admit that she had a night job, that she had no control over her daughter, that Pam was often high on pills, promiscuous, a truant, a liar and a thief. Then the lawyer moved for dismissal on the grounds of the mother's testimony and the judge said "Case dismissed."

At the time I did not realize, as I do now, that our lawyer simply used a typical male trick, the destruction of a woman's character, to win his case. We were so grateful because he got us off that we did not question his tactics. But now I see that all of the women involved here, including Pam's mother, suffered a kind of psychological rape. Ironically, it was the police, not us, who impaired Pam's morals: they threatened to lock her up if she didn't tell her story their way.

This incident happened over ten years ago, but I don't believe things have changed drastically since then. The police still harass lesbians. Perhaps they're more intimidated by us than by straight women because of our independence from men. Recently, for example, a friend of mine was arrested in New York City for being a lesbian. The incident began with an insignificant traffic squabble. Nothing was serious at first. But when the cops heard my friend call the woman with her "baby," they handcuffed her and arrested her. On the way to police headquarters in the car they beat her while she was still handcuffed. At headquarters, there was no camera to be found when it came time to take her mug shots. Quite a coincidence, of course, since her face was badly bruised. If that kind of brutality can happen in New York City, it can happen anywhere.

We cannot depend on the police no matter how *right* we are. Since we cannot expect men to put the same value on our lives as we do, we must learn how to defend ourselves. We are fighting for our lives—a hard and constant struggle. But, as the slogan says, "An army of lovers cannot fail."

CAROLINE FERGUSON

A Long Struggle

Ever since my first homosexual experience at the age of eleven, I had been guilt-ridden by the fact that I was such an oddity. Surely no one else desired women as I did. Other women were not only professing their extreme desire for the male, they were also acting out this *natural* desire. So, being such a unique person, so dirty, so sick, I began to deny my honest feelings and to make an earnest, ruthless effort to become what society said I was meant to be: delicate, passive, physically desirable, and emotionally drawn to men.

I was seventeen, and my efforts to conform seemed to be working. I had met a young man who in fact 'turned me on.' As for those feelings toward women—the deep resurging warmth that would rise from within my vagina when I was with women who attracted me, the desire to kiss them, to move my hands over their bodies, to lie close to them, to bury my face between their breasts, to have sex with them—I hoped they would go away if I didn't act on them.

At nineteen, I was working in a repertory company where I met an actress ten years my senior who took me under her wing. She was a fascinating, maternal woman who had an amazing wit, and I was greatly attracted to her. Her profuse expression of affection for me was something new in my experience. She loved me and had no qualms about this fact. For the first time in my life I loved passionately. She was generous with her money and introduced me to the cultural experiences which would make me sophisticated. She was my woman-mother and I was her woman-child. With her, I shared a free sexual expression: we had made a choice to love each other physically and emotionally—at first so easy. We lived together for three years.

During this time, however, I began to have second thoughts about my homosexuality. Perhaps it was the dominant/submissive character of the relationship that began to erode the love I felt for her, but mostly I think it was the underlying message that a woman *should* find her need for intimacy satisfied with men. I began to feel inadequate again as I had earlier in my life.

I asked myself what I was to do about my weakness. In the hope of assuaging my discomfort, I mixed men into my life with this woman; I could then say to myself, "Well, I am only a 'little' strange." Finally, I left her, knowing that as long as I lived with her she would control me and I would never come to terms with myself. I so wanted to be a *normal woman* who could walk down the street and not feel the need to be discreet lest someone notice that she was 'queer.'

Angry, frustrated, and determined to break from the homosexual lifestyle and all its closeted stress (in the 50s there was no community from which to draw strength, only an isolated existence elaborately hidden from the outside world), I enrolled in college to forget, just forget! I did fairly well at forgetting for the first two years. During my freshman and sophomore years, I moved with a group of Korean veterans whom I found intellectually stimulating. I was relieved to find that they placed no sexual expectations on me: I was 'one of the boys.' As for women, I wished no part of them.

In my sophomore year, I became friends with my English professor. She was outgoing in a quietly reserved way that seemed nonthreatening; and, although I knew I was physically and emotionally attracted to her, and knew also that associating with her would be uncomfortable for me, I decided to allow the relationship to develop. Perhaps I was testing myself: was this desire I had for women lessening in intensity? Could I manage being with women better now? This was to be an intellectual friendship; affection would have no place in our exchange. God, how wrenching that was! Even now, tears well up in my eyes as I remember how cruelly I treated myself in struggling to remain straight and respectable. Nevertheless, I found some meager satisfaction in the fact that I had the strength to want her and yet not act on my feelings. After twenty years I am still close to her; she is the mother figure I need to be complete. The original contract still holds true: there is little display of affection. She knows of my open gayness and supports it, though I suspect she experiences some ambivalence both in her feelings toward me and my feelings toward her. In time this will work itself out.

About a year later, I met a physical education major who was 'interested,' and for a time she succeeded in drawing me out of my closet into a turbulent affair that offered me a needed release. I did not love her. It was only the closeness of her female body that I wanted—nothing more—never allowed her to penetrate me. I was using her. Perhaps we were using each other. After two months, remorse slapped me in the face again, and I abruptly withdrew from the relationship.

Surely there was a place where I could find the strength to live with myself. God! I needed God! After all God does all things. Perhaps He could help me out of my dilemma. Otherwise, I would lose my mind. So, following a period of searching and study and much compromising, and, after confessing my past life and making a firm promise to sin no more, I was accepted into the Roman Catholic Church. It had become clear to me that, if I was to be a good Catholic, I must accept the life of a celibate or marry. I chose to focus only on God and to dedicate my life to religion as a celibate. After college I joined a semi-cloistered order on Long Island to spend the rest of my life in reparation for my base inclinations. Penance . . . a life of penance . . . what else was there for me? The upshot of religious life was that at the end of the gruelling workday, which started abruptly at 5:30 a.m. with the sound of a clanging bell and went on without any breathers until 9:30 p.m., I was exhausted. The highly structured day left nothing to spontaneity, for all decisions were made for me—my part was only to obey. The motto "You, sisters, will accomplish in 15 minutes what it takes 50 minutes to accomplish in the world" represented the fulfillment of this dictum of obedience.

Needless to say, such a regimen left in me no energy for sexual preoccupations. If I had any fantasies, I could choose from a number of penances through which to expiate the abhorrent desires. I was never attracted to any of the women in the convent. One or two were interesting, but the imposed solitude meant we never had an opportunity to get to know each other, and a taboo was placed on "particular friendships." The rationale here was that we had joined a community, and thus no one person should mean more than any other. Jesus Christ was to be the only object of our affection.

Perhaps, too, there was a fear of lesbianism. After a time, I actually began to believe that I had overcome my desire for women, and, when the altarboys (seminarians) began to look good to me, I rejoiced: "It's off my back . . . I am a woman after all!" Marriage and family . . . the great American dream for all red-blooded girls could be mine. After two and a half years, I left the convent to search for a good man.

I took a job in a publishing house in Milwaukee reading manuscripts for syntax and style. There my days were spent very much alone in a sound-proofed room reading manuscripts. Outside of my work I chose to live in isolation, and took a house on a nearby lake. My days were spent driving the 30 miles into the office, working, and driving the 30 miles back to my retreat where I would eat, swim or canoe, and retire early, to rise at 5:00 each morning. During this time I began to date an interesting man. Much to my dismay I was not sexually attracted to him, but I forced myself to respond to his advances. We discussed marriage and, after a time, became engaged. But, at the last moment, I broke it off. He was very sexually aggressive and I found that distasteful. I could not commit myself to him feeling as I did.

I turned my attention to Paul, an editor at the publishing house. We had been working together on manuscripts for some time. I thought him to be such a gentleman, such a good man; he would not be as sexually demanding as the other man I had known—he reeked of respect. I set out to snare him. There was a problem, however; he did not date women. He was intrigued, however, by the fact that I lived in the country, so I invited him out to the lake for dinner. What I went through to make that evening complete! There was a fire, candles on the table, wine chilling in the snow, and stuffed flank steak waiting to be consumed. It worked. We started to date. I was right: he was respectful, a pleasant change from the "clutchers" who so turned me off. This man really loved me for myself. Besides, I had accommmplished the impossible: the confirmed bachelor was mine. One year and a half later I was his wife, carrying our first child. I felt that I could *now* hold my head high. My family was pleased; I was pleased, too, for I had often inwardly agonized: Could I in fact conceive a child, carry a child, and give birth to a child? If I could produce children, then indeed I was a woman. Now I had a husband and a child—who could point a finger at me and ask suspiciously, "Is she a queer?"

For all purposes it was a good marriage. As I had anticipated,

Paul was an entirely devoted and respectful husband and an excellent father. It was I who made most of the sexual overtures. This was an ideal situation because I was never threatened by any 'male aggressiveness' with Paul. Unfortunately, though, I did not get much pleasure from having sex with him, but I resigned myself and inwardly questioned my own adequacies. When we left the Catholic Church, our sex life did improve, but I never experienced the heightened euphoria that I have found in making love with women.

Two children later, I met a woman to whom I was very much attracted, but I chose not to act on my feelings. Our friendship went on without incident, but the pandora's box had been opened slightly. When another woman came along who actively pursued me, I could not resist, and became embroiled in a clandestine affair. This time I did not experience remorse. She did, however, and, pressed down by her feelings of guilt, she lashed out at me and bitterly accused me of seducing her. I was stunned by her coldness toward me. I had shown her nothing but generosity and her behavior left me utterly confused. Hurt and disappointed, I was once again determined never to have anything to do with women, and once more I turned my attention to men. When Paul and I would socialize, I was invariably with the men, laughing and enjoying their banter. I even began to respond to their 'sexual plays'; they knew I had a husband to whom I would be faithful. In the meantime, we could all fantasize. Obviously, this behavior did not endear me to their wives. I suspect I was in fact punishing them. Some of the women attracted me, and, as they were not capable of responding, I would get to them where it would hurt them the most—through their men.

There did come a point, however, when I began relating to another woman in a very consistent long-term way. This was all very closeted and, as far as I knew, hidden from Paul. But, in time, I felt I must confide to him my lesbian feelings and risk the possibility of his rejection; I could not live with the deception. Unknown to Emm, I disclosed to Paul the agony of my double life. His reaction was open and understanding. I was surprised and elated. I went to Emm and told her of my great fortune, to be married to such an understanding man. She was incensed that I had told him about our relationship and accused me of betraying her. If she were ever faced with the question of our involvement, she said, she would deny it. This invalidation of me was devastating, and, for a time, I fell into a deep depression. I knew that I could no longer continue to destroy the best part of my nature. Three weeks in a psychiatric ward brought me to a decision. I would break off sexually with Emm: I could not be her secret. I would come out of the closet. First, I would accept myself, and, second, I would seek out others who shared my sexual orientation. I began to write poetry again for the first time since my undergraduate days. This writing helped me to sort things through by dwelling on my world as I perceived it, rather than as others thought I should. Thus, over time, I clarified many aspects of my life.

Paul came to realize his own homosexuality about a year later, and he is rapidly making his way in the gay world. Though we do not share with each other all the nuances of our lives, we share a great deal and have many mutual friends.

Our children, girls 12 and 16, have been told about our gayness. They understand as well as they can, seem open to it and are not threatened. They accept my lover, Donna, and know that the relationship in no way detracts from my love for them. Paul's friends move in and out of the house with ease. The door is always open; I enjoy their company and count them as my friends too. There is always good conversation to be found over our kitchen table. Our children have experienced caring in the relationship Paul and I have with each other and with the other significant people in our lives, not always agreement, but caring.

Sometimes we think it would be easier on the children if the lifestyle of our family were less frontier-like. There are no precedents for two gay parents. Every day is an experiment, and there is always the unknown, and the ensuing fear that perhaps tomorrow it will ALL FALL DOWN. I doubt if that will happen, however. We are a happy group. The children are self-sufficient and understand their two active, involved parents.

Paul and I will separate within the next few years, when the moment is right for all of us. Divorce is not part of our plan; we are, after all, best of friends.

SANDY BOUCHER

Three Stories

My first story about lesbians was written when I was 24 years old and just married. The year before, I had been involved in a relationship with a woman and I wrote this story to terrify myself, to keep me firmly within a heterosexual lifestyle, to lock the door on my closet, you might say. In order to do this, in the story I had to create a liaison between two women that was so dangerous and so doomed that I would never be tempted to try it again myself. The two women in the story were abstractions taken from what I knew generally about lesbians, plus a little bit of erotic detail which I had picked up firsthand. The story progressed from falling in love, to fear, inner torment, and intimations of disaster—the romantic, tragic (very usual) way of looking at lesbian relationships, at least in stories. And it ended with the suggestion of suicide.

This story was very successful. It really did frighten me a lot. It had served its purpose, and so I put it away. Even though I was writing and publishing stories at that time, this story was meant for my eyes alone. I showed it to no one. The year was 1961. So really I was doing what was possible for me within that historical context—of the late fifties, early sixties.

I had a B.A. in English Literature, but I could do all the reading necessary for that degree and never come across an overtly lesbian character. In Gertrude Stein, in Carson McCullers and Virginia Woolf, there were women who acted rather strangely sometimes, but you would never have been able to say definitely that they were lesbians. I had not read Colette yet, or Proust or Djuna Barnes, or the rest of Virginia Woolf, or Margaret Anderson, or *Psychopathia Sexualis*, or many other writers and books I later came upon.

The gentlest male treatment I can remember was a novel by Robert Kirsch, who was the Book Review Editor of the *L.A. Times*. The central character was an uppermiddle class housewife who was going through some sort of crisis and was having a series of brutal and thoroughly disgusting and humiliating affairs with men. At one point she meets another housewife in her neighborhood who seems to be a decent human being, and happens to be a lesbian, and who invites the central character to be her lover. At which the male author speaks with horror through his character's mind, "Oh no, not that!" and he sends her out into the world for another encounter with a man even worse than the preceding ones.

So this was the context in which that first story was written. You might say it was the "Oh no, not that!" approach to lesbianism.

Ten years later in the early 70s was a different world. And I was a different person. I was no longer married. I had become a feminist and then a lesbian. I had been living for three years in a collective of women and children from which we put out a feminist newspaper and did other political work. I felt connected to and supported by the community of women and the feminist and lesbian writers I knew here in San Francisco.

On a backpacking trip in the Sierras, I began thinking about my first woman lover, the woman I had known before I got married. Hiking along, I began to tell myself the story of who that woman was, how we met, and what we did together. I was trying to bring her back, trying to evoke the real woman just as she had been and the intensity of that experience for me. The activity of hiking in the mountains was woven in and became the frame for the story. As I told it to myself over and over, I became aware that the theme of climbing the mountain was a metaphor for the long and difficult journey I had traveled since I knew that woman. In writing a story called "Mountain Radio"—I accepted this first lover back into my life. Here's a quote from the story to give you an idea of who she was:

> Lenora is a woman of sorrows. We sit in the back of the shop, and we drink tea and she tells me about her life. A long road dotted with stopping places full of anguish, the rest rough and lonely. She is a jewish/catholic 38-year-old reformed-alcoholic dyke who thinks that being a lesbian is the worst misfortune in the world. She is a small and cocky individual permanently barred from the respect of her fellow citizens, whose only satisfying relationship is with her poodle, Anna Pavlova. We sit over our tea and for hours she indulges in her melancholy, talking in a deep caramel voice about lost lovers.

The story was an acceptance of Lenora, and it accorded her the considerable importance she had had in my life. It expressed the joy of our brief knowing of each other and finally acknowledged my identification with her.

So, besides being an account of certain characters and events, and a pondering on various ideas, the story was a political statement, a declaration of loyalties, and a definition of myself as "a woman responsible to myself, having chosen to love women and having opted out of allegiance to and support of, the *Man*." (It's interesting that when "Mountain Radio" was accepted for publication in *Ms.* magazine, the line I just read you was the one line they wanted to cut.)

The third story, called "Retaining Walls," is a sequel to "Mountain Radio." It is about my going back to visit Lenora as she is today. I soon discover that she is no longer the gaunt tragic person she had been (or I had thought she was). She and her lover are two aging dykes, comfortably settled in the suburbs of a Midwestern city. Superficially, it would seem they live much like their straight neighbors, yet there are crucial differences arising from their being two women who love each other. It was the tensions within their outwardly secure and comfortable lifestyle that struck me and that I wanted to investigate in the story, besides my own reaction to the changes in Lenora and the impossibility of finding again what we had had together.

The first two stories I've talked about were self-serving—a working out of urgencies in my own life. In "Retaining Walls," I was more free to serve the story. I cared a lot about Lenora and her lover, and I felt, especially when I began to read the story aloud to groups of women, that in writing as honestly as I could about these women, I had been writing about myself and many of us.

So there has been a progression. The first story was a cautionary tale; the second one, a confrontation with the past and a political statement. Now, with "Retaining Walls," I am committed to an examination of what is in our lives.

NANCY MANAHAN

Lesbian Books: A Long Search

When I was 12, I fell in love. I didn't recognize the symptoms or understand my turbulent feelings. Why? Because my beloved's name was Joanie. Had it been Jimmy or Johnny, I would have known what was happening and rejoiced that my first romantic adventure had begun. But I lived in the world of books and depended primarily on literature as a way of grasping reality. In all my omnivorous reading I had never come across two women in love with each other.

Joanie seemed to love me too, but we never defined our confusing involvement. We had no vocabulary, no romantic conventions which fit. Still, we felt that something was wrong about our attachment to each other. Books, school, parents, church, community told us that our feelings "should" be directed toward boys. Given these pressures, what chance had the emotion between us ever to become anything more than an adolescent crush?

Since Joanie later married, her lesbian involvement may have been merely a phase. For me, it was more. I dated and tried to fantasize about the right man, but my real attractions were to women. By my freshman year in college, although I still hadn't found any depictions of homosexuality in my reading, I began to suspect that the term might have something to do with me.

Finally I checked out all six books listed under "Homosexuality" from the locked shelf of my college library. I was unprepared for what I found. Sick, sordid, depraved wreckages of humanity were paraded through the pages of those abnormal psychology texts. The homosexual case histories revealed gruesome childhoods, psychological (and often physical) deformities and a fondness for sexual acts in public lavatories. The few female homosexuals who were discussed sounded even more revolting than the males.

I compared this information with my own "case history." My childhood had been relatively happy, I possessed no glaring deformities that I had noticed and my biggest sexual thrill had been holding Joanie's hand.

Half of me felt relieved. If that was homosexuality, clearly I had nothing to worry about. The other half of me was terrified. What if I were already tainted and would eventually become as perverted as the creatures in these books? This latter possibility didn't bear thinking about, and the doors of my mind slammed shut to that idea for several years. Majoring in literature did nothing to change my impression of homosexuality; the Great Books I read depicted only female-male relationships as if no other kind existed.

After two years of college I entered a convent, consciously to dedicate my life to a noble ideal, unconsciously to find refuge from my emotional and sexual confusion. While there, I fell deeply in love with another nun, Johanna, who returned my love enough to want to protect me from an orientation she believed could only bring unhappiness. When I left our convent a year later, Johanna urged me to date (I did), marry well (I tried living with him first) and have children (the pill, thank goodness, prevented that).

Then in graduate school two things happened: I became involved with Elsa, a woman who accepted herself as a lesbian; and the women's movement put Simone de Beauvoir's *The Second Sex* in my hands. I pored over Chapter 15, "The Lesbian," where de Beauvoir reassured me that lesbians are not necessarily freaks, alcoholics or unsatisfied spinsters and that they too can have valid relationships. My affair with Elsa, the happiest experience I had known up to then, confirmed what I read, and I began to believe that perhaps lesbianism wasn't a fate worse than death and infinitely more shameful.

Although de Beauvoir has a fondness for phrases like "doomed to homosexuality" and "fated for Sapphic love," she stresses that in our society the male image has been used to represent all that is positive. When women act like human beings they are said to be identifying with men. That had been true of me. I'd had an active childhood, had enjoyed using my body and, since activities on the basketball court and on a horse were hampered by a dress, I rarely wore one after school hours. Naturally, I was labeled a tomboy.

De Beauvoir helped me understand why I had been attracted to "boyish" pursuits and why I had been made to feel guilty for them. Her next point about lesbians hit the target squarely:

"Not admitting male superiority, they do not wish to make a pretense of recognizing it or to weary themselves in contesting it." I liked this idea. In a sexist society why should a woman deal with the oppressor any more than necessary? My choice of women as friends and lovers appeared eminently sensible.

Comforted as I was by de Beauvoir's sociological analysis, I was aware that she'd left out the most important thing: the tremendous emotional and physical charge that vibrated between me and another woman, a charge that had nothing to do with positive or negative identities, that had nothing to do with contesting male superiority. In fact, it had nothing to do with men at all.

To learn more about the emotional aspect of homosexual attraction, I went this time to the graduate library, hoping that its psychology section would provide recent clarifying data. It didn't. But thanks to de Beauvoir, I knew enough to look in the literature section as well. I checked out the classic 1928 lesbian novel, Radclyffe Hall's *The Well of Loneliness* and devoured it that afternoon. I loved every page, not because it was great literature (it isn't) but because, for the first time, I was reading about my infatuations, my fears and conflicts, my guilts, my joys.

Actually I loved the novel only after I got past the first part, which reads like a case history from one of the abnormal psychology texts I had consulted. The heroine, Stephen Gordon, begins with two strikes against her. Not only is she the wrong sex (undaunted, her father gives her the name he has chosen for a son), but also her mother feels repelled by her. Stephen adores her mother Lady Anna. The psychiatrists would conclude that Stephen's first love for a woman was unrequited and thereafter she searched for other women to compensate for that childhood deficit. Or, conversely, they might decide that Stephen's intimacy with her father prevents satisfactory relations with other men because the incest taboo in that first love generalizes to all males. Either route, she would be caught in the analysts' net.

I excused Hall for this prejudiced psychiatric portrait on the assumption that she had been trying to elicit sympathy from a hostile audience by showing that her heroine was not responsible for what she was. (People, of course, did blame Stephen and her creator; in a well-publicized trial, *The Well of Lone-*

liness was condemned as obscene and banned from England.)

Hall herself seems to believe that Stephen Gordon is born, as she puts it, "an invert" and that no damaging childhood experiences were necessary, since her "inversion" is biologically determined. I was not sure where I stood on this issue. On the one hand, I had been trying since childhood to reject the crippling restrictions of "femininity" and to assert myself as a full intellectual and physical being. On the other hand, I felt deep down that I really had no choice; my whole being responded to women in a way it never did with men.

Whatever my uncertainty on this biological point, my life completely validated Hall's description of the consequences: "a life of perpetual subterfuge, of guarded opinions and guarded actions, of lies of omission if not of speech, of becoming an accomplice in the world's injustice by maintaining at all times a judicious silence, making and keeping the friends one respected, on false pretenses, because if they knew they would turn aside . . . ."

Such was the homosexual's dilemma in 1928, and it described mine happening over 40 years later. I was terrified that people would KNOW. Impatiently, I had begun to let my pixie haircut grow out after learning in *The Second Sex* that lesbians typically have short hair. I never mentioned the words "homosexual," "gay," or "lesbian." Inwardly I cringed at people's glances when I walked down the street with Elsa; I was sure the entire faculty saw us arrive on campus the morning after our first night together. To my relief I soon met a fellow graduate student who wanted to be discreet about his homosexuality, and we made a charming couple at required social functions.

The Well of Loneliness helped me identify the causes of my guilty fears and encouraged a budding defiance. Gradually, I refused to let the dread of what my landlady and Elsa's neighbors might be thinking stop me from staying overnight at her house. I didn't yet dare confirm what people might have suspected. That came much later.

Simone de Beauvoir and Radclyffe Hall marked the beginning. I felt annoyed that for years I had struggled with my identity in a vacuum while all the time these two books had lain on a shelf somewhere. Why had I never heard of them? Growing up in a small Midwestern town had contributed to my ignorance, certainly. But, I realized, the church, the educational system, the medical profession, the law had deprived me of my specific literary heritage. I resolved to remedy that deprivation.

During the subsequent months, I searched libraries and bookstores, reading every lesbian book I could find. From the local pornography shop I amassed a collection of cheap paperbacks with titles like *Warped Women*, *Lesbo Hotel* and *My Secret Perversion*. Such trash, I soon discovered, is usually written by men and for men—men who find "two women doing it" more exciting than one.

The graphic purple prose and blatant sado-masochism of these books expressed a male notion of women's sexuality. A typical cover displayed two half-dressed *Playboy* centerfold sirens—precisely the kind of woman I do not find attractive. Only superficial relationships existed between these so-called lesbians, and a favorite formula called for a virile man to rescue at least one woman from the vile perversions of Lesbos. And vile they are. One jacket promised, for example, that these women "were 'gay'—a polite term for the tormenting lust that roiled within them, earning for them the hated name LESBIAN! During the day they seemed normal young women working for a gigantic publishing firm, but at night the violence of abnormal passion sent them writhing into each other's arms."

The violence of abnormal passion had never sent me writhing into anybody's arms, and this genre, I concluded, offered little insight into my identity. Nevertheless, many a midnight found me engrossed in my latest porn shop purchase. While cringing at these books' lurid sexism and just plain bad writing, I felt reassured by all the women making love with each other. It was going on everywhere! Had been for years! I wasn't alone after all! I even reread some of them when I felt the need for a quick reassuring "fix." Where else could I see images—even these miserably distorted ones—of women loving women? (I had not yet discovered the lesbian bars which, when I moved to larger cities, provided the same sort of reassurance.)

Eventually, I was rescued from the porn by Isabel Miller's novel *Patience and Sarah*, published in 1972. Here, at last, was writing that got my approval. Gone were Radclyffe Hall's social pariahs brooding over their fate; gone were the "lesbo hotels" and the "mounds of panting flesh." In their stead was a well-written, humorous, tender love story about women not too different from me. Set in Connecticut around 1816, the novel chronicles the struggles of two young women who, in defiance of their families and their Puritan farm community, choose each other as life partners.

There are some initial similarities between Miller's heroine Patience and Stephen Gordon from *The Well of Loneliness*. Both women were to have been sons. Both revere their fathers and antagonize their mothers. But I felt no irritation with Miller as I had with Hall's crude psychoanalysis. Miller's characters do not illustrate any theory of homosexuality, nor are they tragic freaks of nature. While Radclyffe Hall presents a perfect marriage in Stephen's parents, Isabel Miller—with the heightened consciousness of her time—shows no ideal relationships. She creates in Patience an intelligent, balanced woman capable of choosing unusually, but well, for herself.

Patience and Sarah is a lesbian novel with a happy ending. As such, it was more deeply reassuring than the other books I had read. It also indicated that, though I was mortified that people might suspect Elsa and I were more than "good friends," a more courageous attitude could eventually emerge for me, just as it does for Patience. When confronted with her brother's accusation that she and Sarah are lovers, Patience, terrified of the community censure, lies and renounces her friend.

A year later, however, they come together again and are stronger and braver, ready to commit themselves. For them, being discovered in bed together is no longer the nightmare I personally dreaded. Rather it is an opportunity to confront their horrified families with the truth, then to pack and set off to buy their own farm. Since Miller forgives her heroine's initial denial of love, I could begin to forgive my own wish to do the same.

I began to search for other works that present lesbian characters in a positive, non-exploitative way. One of the best I found, and the one which meant the most to me, was Jane Rule's *This Is Not for You*. This elegant, powerful novel consists of a long letter, never intended to be sent, written by Kate to her friend Esther, who has entered a convent. In the letter Kate tells the story of her silent love for Esther during their many years of friendship and confesses her reasons for rebuffing Esther's own confused love. Kate believes that Esther is heterosexual, that their dispositions are incompatible and that she must protect Esther. But the reader recognizes a more honest reason: a failure of nerve. Kate is loathe to relinquish her shield of noble, self-sacrificing stoicism; she is too much a coward to risk loving Esther openly.

For several years Johanna (who had also left the convent) and I had played out a similar farce. Like Esther, I floundered in conflicting emotions, pulled by this sophisticated woman who fascinated and tormented me, yet pushed by her toward "the good life." *This is Not for You* told me to stop playing an Esther to her Kate.

I flew to San Francisco and announced to Johanna that we were *both* lesbians, that we had been in love for years and might as well admit it, and that life didn't have to be a Greek tragedy. It worked. Johanna stopped trying to protect me from herself, I stopped trying to be heterosexual to please her and today, five years later, we sometimes look across our living room and are gratefully amazed to see each other.

Four books, *The Second Sex, The Well of Loneliness, Patience and Sarah,* and *This is Not for You,* all shaped my identity and helped me make the 17-year journey from a confused infatuation with Joanie to the maturity of a loving partnership with Johanna. If the heterosexual public had read these books as well, I think my journey would have been much easier.

Thankfully the women's and gay liberation movements have made honest lesbian literature a little more available.

But will my young niece see any of the journals and books—fiction and non-fiction—which today offer a more positive lesbian image? I doubt it. Not in her small midwestern town. But she will have an Aunt Nancy and Johanna who, for her 12th birthday, may send her *Patience and Sarah,* with their love.

SUSAN GRIFFIN

Silences

I want to explore the way silences affect a writer's life. In her book *Silences*, Tillie Olsen talks about the effects of material conditions on writers' lives and especially on women's lives, but I want to talk today about psychic silences—silences that occur because of psychic conditions and particularly that silence which affects us as lesbians.

I feel in fact that the whole concept of the muse, or of inspiration, is kind of a cop-out concept. There is something very fascinating going on in the writer's psyche when there is a silence, an inability to write, and it can't very well be explained by "well, today I was inspired" or "it's flowing now."

But in fact, each silence and each eruption into speech constitutes a kind of event and a kind of struggle in the life of the writer. To me the largest struggles in my life around silence had to do with the fact that I am a woman and a lesbian.

When I first recognized my anger as a woman, my feelings as a feminist, suddenly my writing was transformed. Suddenly I had material, I had subject matter, I had something to write about. And then a few years after that I found another great silence in my life. I found myself unhappy with my writing, unhappy with the way I expressed myself, unable to speak. I wrote in a poem—"words do not come to my mouth anymore." I happened also in my personal life to be censoring the fact that I was a lesbian and I thought I was doing that because of the issue of child custody. That was and is a serious issue in my life, but I wasn't acknowledging how important it was to me both as a writer and a human being to be open and to write about my feelings as a lesbian. In fact, I think that writers are always dealing with one sort of taboo or another. If these taboos are not general to society, you may experience in your private life a fear of perceiving some truth because of its implications, and this fear can stop you from writing. I think this is why poetry and dreams have so much in common—because the source of both poetry and dreams is the kind of perception similar to that of the child who thought the emperor had no clothes. The dangerous perception. Dangerous to the current order of things.

But the taboo of lesbianism is loaded for everyone, even for those who are not lesbians. Because the fact of love between women, the fact that two women are able to be tender, to be sexual with each other—affects every event in this society—psychic and political and sociological.

For a writer the most savage censor is oneself. If in the first place, you have not admitted to yourself that you are a lesbian, or to put it in simpler language—that you love women or are capable of wanting to kiss a woman or hold her—this one fact, this little perception, is capable of radiating out and silencing a million other perceptions. It's capable, in fact, of distorting what you see as truth at all.

To give you one example, there have been numbers and numbers of psychoanalytic papers, poems, and articles written on the Oedipal relationship. Everyone seems to recognize that the son can love the mother and that then there is the conflict with the father. This is supposed to be a big taboo and yet everyone can talk about it easily. And yet, who of us really, even lesbians, can talk about the love of the daughter for the mother? Yet all human beings learn love from their mother whether they are male or female. Everyone who's ever been a mother knows that for a fact, a child learns to smile from the mother, learns to enjoy being held. The first love affair, male or female, is with the mother.

I feel that the mother/daughter relationship is one that is central to all women's lives, whether they have made the decision to be heterosexual or homosexual. In fact, when you come to a relationship about the mother and the daughter, you come to a relationship inevitably about the daughter and her own self. If she cannot accept the love she's felt for her mother, if she cannot accept that identification, she cannot accept also the love that she's felt for herself. We get back here to what I think is the central problem with women's writing: that is self-hatred, hatred of the body, hatred of one's own voice, hatred of one's own perceptions. In fact, the female voice is characterized as ugly in this society—especially our mothers' voices. Our mothers' voices are characterized on tv as loud, as harassing, as bitchy, as fish-wifey. Many women, whatever our sexual identification, try to move away from the mother rather than to go back and look at this important relationship. This is only one way in which, as a writer, censoring your feelings of love for women can affect your perceptions.

In fact, I want to tell you the story of a poem that I wrote. I wrote the first line of it a year before the rest of the poem was written. This was a case in which the muse came back a year later, and a real process occurred while she was gone. The poem is called "The Song of a Woman with Her Parts Coming Out." The title occurred to me and the first few lines, but I just simply could not go any further and it was a mystery to me why. It was during a period in which I was in a relationship with a woman whom I loved, but I was not writing about anything in that relationship because I was worried about child custody and because she also was not really willing to call herself a lesbian. And so therefore I couldn't really call myself a lesbian. I couldn't use that word to myself and words are magic. Shakespeare understood word magic. In *King Lear* just the simple "nothing" changed everyone's life in that play. Words have a tremendous power and I believe that it is extremely important to use that word, to be able to say: I am a lesbian.

The result of this poem did come out when I reexamined this in myself and decided that indeed I had to use that word. I had to be open about my sexuality in my writing . And I'll end with that poem, "The Song of a Woman with Her Parts Coming Out."

> The song of the woman with
> the top of her head ripping off, with
> the top of her head ripping off
> and she flies out
> and she flies out
> and her flesh flies out
> and her nose rubs against her ass,
> and her eyes love ass
> and her cunt
> swells and sucks and waves,
> and the words spring from her mind
> like fourth of July rockets,
> and the words too come out,
> lesbian, lesbian, lesbian, pee, pee, pee, pee, cunt, vagina,

dyke, sex, sex, sex, sex, sweat, tongue, lick, suck, sweet,
sweet, sweet, suck,
and other words march out too,
the words,
P's and Q's
the word
nice
the word
virginity,
the word
mother,
mother goodness mother nice good goodness good good
should
should be good be mother be nice good
the word
pure
the word
lascivious
the word
modest
the word
no
the word
no
the word
no
and the woman
the woman
the woman
with her
parts coming out
I am bleeding
the blood seeps in red
circles on the white
white of my sheet,
my vagina
is opening, opening
closing and opening;
wet, wet
my nipples turn rose and hard

my breasts well against my arms
my arms float out
like anemones
my feet slide on the wooden
floor,
dancing, they are dancing, I sing,
my tongue slips from my mouth
and my mind
imagines a
clitoris
I am the woman
I am the woman
with her parts coming out
with her parts coming out.

never stopped
never stopped
even to
say yes,
but only
flew with
her words
with her words
with her words
with her parts
with her parts
coming
with her parts
          coming
          coming
          coming
          out.

MARGARET CRUIKSHANK

A Conversation with May Sarton*

Margaret Cruikshank: The last time you were in the Bay Area, you certainly got a warm reception from audiences.

May Sarton: I have a warm reception everywhere I go. This is not news. In St. Paul, just last week, they set up closed circuit TV for 200 people who couldn't get into the hall.

MC: At the University?

MS: No, at the Unitarian church. They gave me their Ministry to Women award. I'm very in with the Unitarians.

MC: Did you miss the great blizzard?

MS: Yes, but there was still snow on the ground. I took my boots. It's such beautiful country. I love all the lakes. At night from the plane they look black among all the lights.

MC: Did you have any time in St. Paul to see the nuns at St. Catherine's?

MS: Yes, I saw Sister Maristella, who now calls herself Sister Alice—I can never get it right. We had a long talk. I love that place. I feel very much at home in the Catholic colleges. The most radical women today are nuns. I can be absolutely open.

They gave me their Alexandrine Medal. And the woman who introduced me, at a formal dinner, Sister Mary Virginia, was dressed in a white cowboy pants suit with a pink bow. And I had spent miserable hours trying to find an evening dress. I never wear dresses. Here I was looking immensely fat in a horrible evening dress. And here she was looking very comfortable in what I would have rather been wearing.

MC: A wonderful story.

MS: The nuns are radical but everything is grounded in a spiri-

*A shorter version of this interview was published in The Advocate, August 18, 1983.

tuality. Those two things go well together for a poet.

MC: There is a sense of beauty on the campuses. And the nuns respect creative women. At my college, the woman artist was taken as natural.

MS: Exactly.

MC: Does the warm reception for you everywhere now ever get boring?

MS: Never, because I'm seventy now and it's taken sixty years for this to begin. So I feel not the tiredness of the long-distance runner but the elation of the long-distance runner who really finally gets there.

MC: I guess a question behind my question is, do you feel less challenged now?

MS: The challenge is that I still have not had serious critical attention from the literary establishment. Where I'm taught is in women's studies. Occasionally in an English department. But I'm not in the canon of the teaching of literature anywhere in the country. A woman wanted to do a dissertation on me, and the professor said, "Who is May Sarton?" as if I were somebody in the bushes she'd pulled out. I think of Sinatra's song, "I've Done It My Way."

MC: That's true.

MS: I have huge audiences now simply because the books are human and reach people of all ages and all kinds. People at the colleges where I read are amazed by the huge audiences, but the people come from the small villages on the prairie, in the case of Minnesota. Women just pour in who know my work, who perhaps never went to college. That's the thing I love. On the other hand, I'd love also to get some recognition from the critics. Maybe that will never happen. It doesn't matter now.

MC: No, because of your audience.

MS: And because they care. For years, when I was young, when I sat down at my desk, I used to think I should be in the slums working with Black kids or in Africa. I always had this conflict between art and life. I'd fight this out every morning and think,

well, maybe the work will have, in the end, something as valuable as if I were working in a hospital or in the slums. Now I
know that the work *has* helped a great many people. So that
conflict is greatly eased. That's partly an answer to your question, what is it like to be seventy? At last I feel useful. I know
I'm useful. I don't have to worry about doing something else. I
have to worry about doing what I do as well as I can, which is
a great anxiety for any writer.

MC: Did you feel the life/art conflict as a very young woman
when you were part of the theater?

MS: No, because the theater, of course, is a place of giving. Eva
LeGallienne's motto was, the theater is an instrument for giving,
not a machinery for getting. We had a $1.65 top price, which
even in the thirties was very low. Fifty cents in the second
balcony. And I was writing poems. I never stopped writing
poems after I was ten years old. My first poems came out in
Poetry Magazine when I was at the Civic Repertory. I remember
showing them to Eva LeGallienne with great pride. I was eighteen. I knew I was a poet very young. I think any poet does.

MC: But you felt useful in the theater.

MS: And I fell in love with that theater. I was wide-eyed. I'm
glad I never went to college. I think it would have made me
into a bluestocking. I think things out but I'm not an intellectual.
I would have been given a kind of intellectual machinery in
college which I think I've done well not to have.

MC: Having gone, I think I understand.

MS: And, of course, I came from an academic family. My father
was a great scholar. I was brought up in Cambridge, Massachusetts, and all that. The theater brought me in touch with
all kinds of people I never would have known had I gone on
in the academic world.

MC: Like Woolf, you were in the milieu.

MS: Yes. When you don't go to college you read only what you
want to. So you find the food that you need at that moment in
your life. I found Simone Weil at a certain time . . . and Tillich.

MC: You had wonderful teachers, too.

MS: Yes, before I went to high school. Poetry was the thing that was most alive at Shady Hill School because the head of the school was a crazy, wonderful Irishwoman, Alice Hocking. For her poetry was the reality, and we were brought up to believe that. To recite it. To learn by heart. To talk it. To feel that it was our own world.

MC: In your writings you say that you feel lucky in having had that kind of school.

MS: Extremely lucky. Shady Hill School made me what I am. It gave you the tools to do whatever was in you. It was a so-called progressive school, but it was really very disciplined. The standards were very high. You weren't allowed to get away with careless work.

MC: That's an ideal.

MS: For me it still is.

MC: An unusual combination of discipline and liberation.

MS: The ego must be constantly disciplined by the subject. That's something I find lacking in a great deal of poetry that's written today. A great deal of what I read seems to me very self-indulgent, as if the writer had not learned anything from writing the poem, whereas I feel my poems teach me what has really been happening.

MC: Openness to revision, is that it?

MS: Yes. God gives one something to work with. There's always something given. It doesn't mean that's it.

MC: I like what you say about form not being an inhibitor, not stopping the creativity but allowing it to be expressed.

MS: You see, I cannot use form unless I'm inspired. It's far from being something you paste on. I can't write in form unless I'm working at white heat. You're more critical when you're inspired than any other time. Your mind also is working very fast and well, and in the groove, and you're choosing one word and throwing out another. That's the critical faculty. I revise sometimes sixty times. "In Time Like Air," which I'm reading tonight [at College of Marin] I think went through about sixty drafts. It's a very tight form; it's a metaphysical idea, hard to work out; it had a marvelous image. You get the poem when you have three things: one, something has hit you where you live, as they say. You're really struck by something so you're in an exceptionally aware state. Then the subconscious brings you an image. The third thing for me—musical lines run through my head, I mean lines in meter. And when those three things are present, I get a really good poem. If they're not, I get only what Louise Bogan used to call an imitation poem.

MC: I remember your opinion that being a poetry critic for so many years was harmful to her art. Are you glad that you didn't have to do that?

MS: Well, I did, of course. I used to review for *The Saturday Review*, for *The Times*. I felt I didn't want to be a critic of other people's work, only of my own. I think it's very dangerous. There's so much power involved. It's very dangerous for creative people to have power. It's the antithesis of creation.

MC: Especially that kind—the power to condemn, to dismiss.

MS: Exactly. You see this—the crowing over something great by some tiny little person who is nothing.

MC: It sets up a false equation between the creative writer and the critic.

MS: Yes, and each person really sees a work differently.

MC: Recent books that excite you?

MS: I've just been reading a really wonderful first novel by Jane Somers, apparently a well-known English journalist who uses that as a pseudonym. The book is called *The Diary of a Good Neighbor*, and I picked it up in the women's bookstore in Berkeley. It's about a very smart, professionally successful woman who has no heart and who is absolutely changed by a sort of fortuitous collision with an old, dirty, miserable sick woman, whom she finally really takes care of. It's marvelously well done. That relationship was just overwhelming to me. I cried and cried when I finished the book. I felt, thank God someone has realized this—the humanization of a person by dealing with old age at its most repulsive. The fierce light in this old woman, the fierce will to live! [Doris Lessing later revealed that she had written *The Diary of a Good Neighbor*.]

MC: Other recommendations?

MS: The *Letters* of Sylvia Townsend Warner. And Judith Thurman's *Life of Isak Dinesen*, which is a masterpiece. It's interesting to talk about this because many people now want to write my biography. I don't want it done until I'm dead. I'd want everything to be told, and there are people alive. . . It's got to wait. What you get from Thurman's biography is an overall view which is both kind and detached, but which came, undoubtedly, out of a passionate involvement with the woman after she was dead. Thurman learned Danish; she went to Africa. But then she was somewhat disillusioned, I think, and then she got this whole view. I'd like her to do my biography. I wrote her a fan letter. She's quite young. Thirty-five or so.

MC: It's wonderful to feel that respect for a biographical work at the point where you'd be thinking of your own biography.

MS: She has a real style. Very economical. It's highly intelligent. It's much better than Glendenning's biography of Elizabeth Bowen. The fault in that book is that you don't really want to read Bowen after you read Glendenning. Never mind. She gave quite a good review to *A Reckoning*.

MC: Well, who would be good candidates for your biographer?

MS: I would be very wary of a biographer for myself who was too into the literary world, who knew everybody. This is not what I want.

MC: It's funny to think of you *sending* a fan letter. I'll bet Thurman was pleased.

MS: Yes, she was very pleased. Another great book of the last ten years is Shirley Hazzard's *The Transit of Venus*. Magnificent. Marvelously well written. That's so rarely true of lesbian literature. It doesn't have sufficient detachment. Maybe I'm wrong. Maybe I haven't read enough. But I'm somewhat put off by a lot of what's being written. For instance, I don't feel that the clitoris is any more worth emphasizing in love poems for a woman than a penis. I would find this equally repulsive. Love poems should be essences, not physical. Maybe it's partly that the lesbian is just coming out, that she can now say these things she could never say before. In a novel, I don't like physical descriptions of sex. They do nothing for me.

MC: Maybe our politics and our anger have interfered with our prose style, our sense of craft?

MS: Yes, I think so, to some extent. Anything homosexual will be taken by the homosexual magazines whether it's good or not. And so much is badly written, self-indulgent. The anger is all right. But it should be expressed in a literary way. You have to think, will someone read this five hundred years from now? Will it stand up? That's what literature is all about.

MC: Or even ten years.

MS: Or even ten years.

MC: Then we'd toss a lot of stuff in the wastebasket.

MS: Yes, we would.

MC: The gay magazines are limited to those writers who are openly gay enough to be published in them. That may exclude some of the better writers.

MS: I was pleased to see that the author of *Rubyfruit Jungle* had a full-page ad in *The Times*. Now evidently she really has a name which is generally known.

[The talk turned to a sense of community among women writers.]

MS: I miss very much having a community. I've never had one and maybe I never will. I can see that it must be very good and very supportive to have it.

MC: It might be intrusive sometimes.

MS: The nice thing about being seventy is you can say you're too old.

MC: You mean, too old to be bothered?

MS: Too old to do your own work and stuff envelopes for a writers' group.

MC: But readers of your books would have an impression of your vigor?

MS: I met a young woman at a reading I gave in Charlotte, NC. She was absolutely unprepared for an older person because she discovered me through *Journal of a Solitude.* The shock must have been great. I had to wear a dress on that occasion, which I hate to do, and I looked very ladylike, I think, and she was quite put off. By the end, she said, "You looked like a fortress," which dismayed me.

MC: In an interview in the Constance Hunting book *May Sarton: Woman and Poet,* you say that you do not intend to write a lesbian novel.

MS: No. I think of myself as a bridge between the homosexual world and the heterosexual world.

MC: I want to ask about your novel *Faithful Are the Wounds,* one of my favorites.

MS: I'm so glad you like it. I was at Harvard with F. O. Matthiessen and he couldn't have been nicer to me. Of course, I was in a very lowly position—for three years I taught freshman English.

The one problem with the book is that I knew nothing about his private life. He was homosexual, of course, and lived for years with Russell Cheney, a painter. Everybody knew that but me. I do suggest, I think, that something about him made him different from other people.

The reason I wrote the novel was that about six months after his suicide, which made us all feel guilty, I began to hear "Poor Matty; he couldn't take it." At this time, before World War II, it was the fashion at Harvard to be detached. We were just beginning to know how bad it was in Germany. Matty was totally involved and committed. The attitude of the people who didn't care was that he couldn't take it. Maybe he couldn't take it because he cared.

It was overwhelming to him when it was proved in Czechoslovakia that the Socialists and the Communists could not work together. The Communists took over. At first I wanted to show only the effect of his suicide and not have him on the stage himself. Then, as I wrote, I realized he had to be there, alive on the page. I think that choice made the book much better, but it also laid me open to the criticism later that he was not homosexual in the book and should have been.

MC: But in those days gay people were so private.

MS: Yes, but since then of course Matthiessen's letters to Cheney, including love letters, have come out. I was hated at Harvard because of *Faithful Are the Wounds*. They thought that because Cavan is obviously Matthiessen, everybody in the novel was somebody in the English department. But I made up all the characters. I went to great lengths to do so. Damon Phillips is Julian Huxley—nobody could possibly have known that. Harry Levin decided that he was Goldberg. I'm anathema to him. He says the book is of no consequence and nobody should read it.

MC: I like the political seriousness of the novel. It shows how liberals who make moral choices can get isolated. I learned some history from it.

MS: Matthiessen and I were on the board of directors of the Civil Liberties Union. That part came from experience. He came to parties at my house. And he was so much like a wounded bear in his last days. I knew he was unhappy. I didn't know about Cheney. [Matthiessen's lover had died.]

MC: That relationship has been described recently by Eric Rofes in a book on gay suicide.

MS: Yes, I read that book. Quite good.

MC: Maybe it will create new interest in *Faithful Are the Wounds*.

MS: A man from Harvard who's writing the definitive biography of Matthiessen, whose name is White, came to see me and said that my book is absolutely wonderful and very true. I was so relieved. This was the first kind word I've had from Harvard in thirty years. Harvard is still very backward about women.

MC: Elitist schools have been the most resistant to women's studies.

MS: And even schools like Princeton, where there are women students, haven't done much about the faculty.

MC: Going on to Mrs. *Stevens Hears the Mermaids Singing*—at one point the main character, Hilary, suggests that homosexuality is not as good a choice as heterosexuality. I wonder about your own view. Surely it's easier to be heterosexual.

MS: No, I think it's very much harder to be heterosexual, from the inward point of view. It's easier from the social, outer point of view. Of course, I am a lesbian. But if you are a heterosexual woman, you are taking the stranger in; you are taking into you, even physically, somebody very different from you. A woman knows exactly how the other woman feels; you know how to make love to a woman without being told. And then living with a woman you also know the needs of a woman. On the social level it is much harder to be a lesbian. Now there are communities where women can feel less isolated. Nowadays, with my small fame, I'm not invited to dinner parties because it's not convenient to have a single woman. I don't want to be—except occasionally—this is no grief to me. Any widow quickly learns that she's not asked out as much. This is not true with artists but in the social world. I meet women who are lovers in towns all over the country who can't ever come out. Sometimes one of them is married, and they have a very hard time. I have great sympathy for them. Gay men are invited out a lot in a way that gay women are not, in the square world, or whatever you call it. There's always room for another man at the table.

MINNIE BRUCE PRATT

In Which I Weep Like Niobe

9/11/75

I will shrivel up like the sauteed onions and squash we ate
if I have to sit through another family meal like last night's,
with M taping "You don't even listen to a word I say" into
R's rebellious ear and my sitting silent, silent. I feel a coward
for not fighting M on the lesbian mother issue through the
streets and into the courtroom in the mother battles like tigress
for her children routine: but I already feel I have lost them.
My sons R and B will bracket me as 'mother' and have smash-
em-up fantasies about me, their own Punch and Judy show.
I know now that I cut communication with M because he is
male, because he doesn't hear me even when he listens, yet
I long to keep a line on two boys who at 5 and 7 are merely
pre-pubescent patriarchs. Yesterday the Junior Service League
had a "feminist" speaker who justified women's liberation
because it would help men and children in the long run: trash
from the same receptacle as the Renaissance argument that
women should be educated because then we would be better
mothers. I slept with S for myself; I work in the Movement
for myself and that self in other women, for that female self
which was conceived and born in my male children but which
dies with every year of their growth toward manhood. Yet I
can hardly face toward my own leaving and deliberately leaving them behind in M's world. I still feel them to be my babies,
those selves rolled in the flesh of my womb, even though they
were mine for only these few years, or perhaps were never
mine.

9/15/75

A dream: the boys and I are swimming in a muddy creek,
with sharp currents of warm and cold water, like Schultz creek
in my childhood. There are sudden drops and I warn them of
the danger. Getting out on the other side, we meet groups of
women; we have no place to stay and I feel awkward about
asking any of the women for help: social embarrassment on the

other side of the Jordan. After the Revolution, what do I do with my boy children?

9/18/75

I spent Tuesday evening with S after a mud and acid bath from M. Being with her in that clear stream of love washed away some of the despair. We listened to Brodsky on tape and made love slowly, my hands slipping down to her knees, my hair rubbing, brushing her hair, kissing her.

Denying all the while his revulsion at my love affair with S, nevertheless M is reworking his icon of the Constant Wife into a caricature of the Crazy Lesbian. When I requested an equal split of debts and cars, he threatened to close the joint checking account, leaving me penniless for three weeks until my first check from school comes. He says, "As the man I'm responsible for the debts; you are being irresponsible." When I refuse to talk to him when he threatens me, he says, "You have to communicate more or I won't let the boys go with you." When I become angry or anxious about arrangements with the children, he says, "You have been acting rather strange, funny, possessed." When I said that I didn't believe in this male-headed family for myself or for the children, he sneered, "Then are you going to tell your family, your mother about S?"

9/25/75

I'm down deep, inside a diving-bell of depression. S and I had another fight which she ended by saying that I treated her like M treated me; I was just like a man. My first check from school was cut 30% for taxes, so I don't know if I can leave M before November. But more shaking than doubts about love and money is my fear of the effect of my leaving on the children.

M has finally succeeded in making me feel guilty about something: that I don't care for the children because I haven't talked with him about how to prepare them for the separation. The moment has to come, but I can't stand to cause them pain. What will it be for them, those four nights and days a week when I won't be there? They are already saying, "Will you be here tonight?", or "I don't want M to yell at me about my clothes before school tomorrow; will you be here to dress me?" I feel that I am leaving them without a comforter for their bad dreams, and without a confidante for bad days. I don't see how I can leave, but I have to. It is as logical for me to leave M as it was for me to marry him. I have outgrown dependence on him as I outgrew prayers to a Presbyterian Father. But the very inevitability of being alone is frightening.

10/12/75

My heart is crushed by fury at my lover. After telling the children that, like our stories of the two boys who lived alone in the woods, I was to have a house of my own, I went over to see S. Talking to the children numbed me, with R screaming "no, no" and B adrift in his six-year-old world. We drove over to my house, and they scrambled about for a while, frantically shoving and pushing drawers, light switches; then they went back to M's to bed. At S's, I told her each comment in babbling detail and, I suppose, irritated her with my obvious distress over them. When I asked her to hold me for a little warmth and said I loved her, I was told, "Don't say those words to me." She is too quick with me now; the pain of the children hurts me so and I need comfort. I am bodiless, headless, heartless with anger and grief; I think for the first time in months, of lying down with M for the warmth of his back: how impossible a comfort.

11/4/75

Since I moved out two weeks ago, and after the NOW convention with S in Philadelphia, I have felt more M's attempt to control me with the children. He has announced that I am to have them at Thanksgiving, but he will probably drive with them to my mother's house for Christmas. I indicated, as calmly as I could through a red fog, that if anyone went down with them to Alabama to see my mother, I thought that I should. M replied, "Well, you can come, if you want to."

In M's moebius logic, I have forfeited, by my distaste for Man's institution of marriage, by my sexual autonomy, by my love for women, any claim for recognition in the eyes of the people who bore and raised me. He becomes the son my mother never had, and I the prodigal daughter, who can only return by the side of her husband. M constantly reproaches me as the outsider, the unnatural one, the abnormal who left, who must adapt to his pattern, to that of the 'family'—but I can drop in anytime I want.

His rage at my sexuality spewed out on Halloween when I

went over to treat with the boys and bring them back to spend the weekend with me. I planned to go out later after they were asleep and had dressed up. Noting my velvet coat, M sternly withdrew his permission for their visit; if I was to be so irresponsible and careless of them as to get a sitter, I could not have them over. They were his family and he was responsible for their well-being. To his unctuousness, smooth as baby-fat, I replied, "You are trying to possess the kids; they don't belong to anyone but merely have two parents; you will ruin them by this control, this vampire act." Then the stones fell: "Go fly all over the country with your queer lover if you want to, but shut up and do what I say now or get out and come back when you can talk like a civil person." I refused to go and refused to shut up so he grabbed, shoved, and slammed me into the corner of the kitchen by the stove, which was fortunately not on, and then he threw me out the door onto the cement back porch. During those few seconds, I screamed thoroughly, and thought: This is very like a scene from 'Woman Under the Influence' and also: I will scream so the boys know that I am being hurt and that M is the one hurting me. And I thought as I hit the cement with my back: He might kill me. However, the knives, for once, had been put away in the utensil drawer.

Furious, I hopped up, with my left knee and elbow and right hand bleeding a bit through the black velvet, and jumped back into the kitchen to refuse again to leave. The boys saw all of this and were screaming also. B, standing between me and M, told him to stop and slapped M in the face; R shrank back into the dining area, dazed, clearly seeing that M had won. M, shouting, but in character in his righteous rage, fulfilled the destiny of his stereotypical soul: "You goaded me into this; you are trying to rationalize your leaving me by making me hit you." This male obtuseness still astonished me: I suppose my stiff elbow and darkening bruises are inventions of my diseased imagination.

11/19/75

I'm inundated with tears and letters, from married friends, from aunts, mother, grandmother. My friends tell me how wonderful their marriages are; my mother can't understand how I can be so selfish as to abandon M and the children; my 96-year-old grandmother prays for my soul and urges a psychiatrist. I don't think I can ever go home and see any of them again.

Re-reading Jill Johnston's "Return of the Amazon Mother," which is right about people's non-acceptance of a mother giving up her children, I have been suffering and grieving for them and for myself, for my not being free of M, for my not having the boys, for the impossibility of honest love, since to be open about my lesbianism would mean that they could be taken from me legally. I loathe having to be careful what and who the children see when they are with me. Last summer I had searing fights with M over whether they would see S; I gave in, when I understood that he wouldn't leave for Harvard, and leave me alone for a month, unless I 'swore' not to 'expose' them to her. Now, terrified about giving him an excuse to refuse them to me altogether, I have to be careful about all my friends. Most of M's literary friends are male and gay but, as M so intelligently puts it, "The children don't see them doing anything illegal," while R and B have actually seen S and me kiss and hold hands.

And now the fear about the children has frozen that lovely, sensuous feeling that I had first for S. She feels that; she is afraid of sex with me. I am too coldly separate, like a dead woman, or too angry, burning up myself and anyone near me.

11/25/75

I had thought I'd gone to the bottom, but last night was mud. Ill and aching with the flu, I called my mother from the Cross Creek pay phone. She said, "If the family collapses, so does society," in her usual Southern voice of doom, and refused to come to see me during Christmas, and refused to forbid M to bring the children down there without me. And refused to acknowledge my pain and ache of betrayal that she, my mother, has chosen to please him, rather than comfort me, her daughter.

I can see the Christmas to come: everyone, O.G., Evie, Lethean, all the aunts, Mama, Grandma, the cousins, Bobby, Jack, Mary, their wives and husbands, all there for sweet potatoes with marshmallows, jello salad, with third generation cousins rolling around, Michael and two Christophers, Laura, R and B. They sympathize with M over his crazy wife, and he moves through the crowded house, more confident of his righteousness, saving the family: mine.

12/17/75

The children are with me while M goes off to Durham; evidently I become normal when he wants me to baby-sit. I'm nervous with R and B, afraid of them, afraid of hurting, not pleasing. R cried as we left daycare because we were to get a Christmas tree for my house; he wanted me and the tree to be in Alabama with them, or wanted to take the tree to M's house. After we decorated, they stayed up late, playing and fighting. I yelled at them, we fell exhausted in bed, all three of us finally, with R holding my hand. What are we all to one another?

12/22/75

Three days ago on B's birthday he seemed so unlikely an inhabitant of my swollen belly six years ago; B and I made a cake and cut it with M and R. As I left, M toasted me with his bourbon, "It's our ninth anniversary; don't you remember?" A victory of detachment at last: I didn't. He asked plaintively, "Are you coming to Alabama?" Yesterday they drove off in the van crammed with presents.

Since Christmas in Alabama now means to me the convergence of tradition, religion, and emotion around my neck in the smooth collar of matrimonial reconciliation, I called my mother last night from the pay booth down the road and said that I was not coming. Trembling and frozen in the open booth, I heard my mother crying at the other end, B anxious, R angry, M silent.

After the call, I had a winter solstice party, with women, talk, wine, Meg Christian, politics. I watched S and she caught me wanting her, and held my foot. I think I learn from S because she listens to her own self, her body, her ideas, and fights for them; I have ignored mine so now I must listen to my self.

But to hear that self is hard when my mother is whispering, "You must consider others to live. Go back to your family," when I know her ideal of unselfish duty, that martyrdom, is all my past life of Southern consideration, womanly consideration. When my children cry, "You are selfish. Hold us," it is hard to turn from their warm and transient caresses to embrace that steadfast self.

SHARON E. BUDD

Proud Lesbian Motherhood

My journey to proud lesbian motherhood has been a long one, sometimes painful, often difficult. It has involved some hard decisions, a few I now regret but which perhaps were necessary for me and for the special relationship I have with my daughters.

I am a thirty-six-year-old graduate student in a counseling program at Kansas University. My daughters, Jackie, 12, and Jennie, 11, may soon live with me again. Because I could not support them, they have lived with their father for the past three years. I see them frequently during the week and they stay with me a couple of weekends each month. I have been out to them for two and a half years, although I'm sure they knew I was different long before I told them I was a lesbian. They accept me and we are all very close—special people to each other.

I have not always appreciated being a mother, however, or a mother of daughters. From the time I knew I could have children I wanted boys, lots of them. I think this was because I so identified with the male role in my younger days, when I realized that males were more valued in this society.

By the time I was a high school senior, in the early sixties, I had had years of lesbian fantasies, culminating in a brief, very exciting but also disturbing affair with a young school teacher who was well known in my community, and whose strong religious convictions caused us both pain, doubt and anguish. Another scare came from not knowing much about what our love meant except that it was not "normal" or accepted. Also, in my small, isolated hometown in the Northwest there was nowhere to go and no one to turn to for support and information. So when I came to college in Kansas I decided to squelch my feelings for women and try to become attracted to men: I dated a few classmates, went to dorm parties, and accepted blind dates arranged by girlfriends when I spent vacations at their homes. Also, I would participate in the obligatory "necking" sessions, but that's as far as I'd ever go with a man before my marriage. I decided to marry at the end of my junior year partly because I was in love, partly for security, and mostly because I knew this was right. Then I decided to have kids, not because I'd ever been especially fond of children, but again because it was part of a married woman's role.

With the birth of my first daughter I felt disappointment but I loved her as my child and I knew I could try again for a son. When I learned my second child was also a girl I felt intense disappointment, anger, and also guilt—guilt because I hadn't yet produced a boy, but also because all these feelings weren't fair to my new daughter. (Now I realize how much I had bought the "males are better" line and I'm still angry at having to go through all that.) Fortunately those feelings passed and both my girls became very precious to me, although I still had ambivalent feelings about motherhood.

After five years of marriage I started to acknowledge that I was not happy: something was missing; some very real feelings, long buried and denied, were pushing for release. I found an understanding male therapist who suggested I acknowledge my lesbian feelings. What a relief! But then we moved and my next therapist (also a male) tried to make me feel guilty. He encouraged me to accept my "proper" role as a woman. With much effort I managed to survive that "therapy" and finally after ten years of marriage I got a divorce.

About this time I had my second lesbian relationship and though my husband was suspicious, I think, he never tried to use my lesbianism to get custody. I know I am lucky that he didn't. We were awarded joint custody and during the next year Jackie and Jennie lived with me. My lover was around often and we decided not to hide our affection. I wanted my daughters to know I *could* be happy with someone—for me this meant with another woman. More important, I thought they should know that I was not ashamed of this relationship. Although at the time we didn't discuss the implications of my new life, the girls really seemed to accept my changes. They liked Nancy very much. She was somewhat younger than I, outgoing, fond of animals, and she enjoyed spending time with Jackie and Jennie. They seemed to assume our love was natural and they weren't threatened by it. One indication of this acceptance was an "association" game we often played where one person would say "hot," and the other person, "cold," etc. Once, Jackie said, "Mommie," and Jennie replied, "Nancy." My lover and I were surprised and pleased with this reaction.

Despite the fact that I was happier now as a lesbian, I still had many things to work out. I was teaching high school but felt unhappy in this career. I was also feeling stifled in the community and needing to find new experiences and new people. Although we tried to work on our relationship, my lover and I found we had unresolvable conflicts and we parted.

Some friends who had been in the Army suggested that joining the service might be a way for me to travel, to learn a new career and to meet interesting people, perhaps many lesbians. After much soul-searching, I did decide to leave my kids with my ex-husband to join the Army. Of course I did not find much support for this move. Society said, "How can you run off and desert your daughters?" Most of the lesbian community said, "How can you run off and leave your daughters with their father?" I have not yet completely resolved some of the guilt about that decision but it did not prove disastrous. My former husband is not an ogre but a good man who loves his kids very much and they have been happy with him.

During my first weeks in the Army, at basic training, I felt very lonely and frustrated; I had expected that most of us there would be lesbians, but in my platoon of forty women, the majority were straight, or so I thought. It would have been difficult to make contact with other lesbians there in any case, since the military, especially at that stage, insures that new recruits understand that homosexuals are not welcome and will be discharged if discovered. At my permanent post in the Northwest, however, I was able to meet many lesbians, though generally not on post. We usually met at downtown bars or at private parties. After a few months I met someone special at a bar; she was assigned to an adjacent company. Shortly thereafter we moved into a house together, off base.

While we were living together my kids came for a visit and I decided then to come out to them. At that time they were ten and eight. I thought this openness was something we all needed and I also wanted to tell them myself before someone else told them in a negative way. The topic evolved naturally in a conversation about the facts of life: who can have babies, who can't;

who can marry, who can't. I explained that there are some men who love each other and some women who do, too, and that they are called homosexuals, or gay men, and lesbians. Long pause. "I've decided it's time for you to know I'm a lesbian, and so is Mary. We love each other and we think of ourselves as married. This makes me different from the other moms you know, but it doesn't change at *all* how I feel about you. You are my very special girls and always will be. I love you both so much and that won't ever change. . ."

Reply: "It's OK, Mom. We know that you're a neat mom and we love you too." What relief! Can't beat that response. They had many questions, which I answered. I also felt I had to tell them that many non-gay people think gays are bad and that it's wrong to be gay. Because of this prejudice, I warned them, we might face some hassles. I didn't want to scare them, I just wanted them to hear about reality and to be prepared for any future adverse reactions.

Although I liked my Army job and had made many good friends, I found after two years that I could no longer tolerate the oppressive, threatening atmosphere of the military. Friends told about the awful experience of being investigated, where they were pressured to reveal not only their own homosexuality but also the names of other suspected lesbians. I also heard accounts of women agents who would try to trap suspected lesbians by pretending to be lesbians themselves. Occasionally obvious agents (men) would infiltrate our bar and at one point, the bar was put off limits to military personnel.

I really didn't want to live with the fear of being discovered nor did I want to tolerate discrimination anymore. Also, my lesbian-feminist identity and consciousness were growing stronger and I felt I needed to get out of the service and to live honestly. By then I had met several proud gay people who were openly political and I was reading about many others. I was greatly inspired and motivated by their courage and honesty. Another source of strength and support was a C-R group I had joined. Members were both gay and straight women and all of them supported my decision.

Another factor in my choosing to leave the military was my children: I was *really* missing them and I couldn't get stationed closer to them. So I went to my superiors and told them I wanted to get out of the Army—that was another dramatic coming out. Fortunately I had a lot of good advice from friends who had also got out as gays, and from sympathetic clerks who handled this type of dismissal. They cautioned me to tell the authorities and psychiatrists (an interview with them is a required part of the procedure) that I had lesbian *tendencies* only; I could not admit to prior or present activity. I feel lucky that I left with an Honorable discharge instead of a Dishonorable or even a General discharge. The Honorable entitles me to receive all the benefits of military service. The Dishonorable, of course, does not provide these; it also labels the *person* dishonorable and makes it extremely difficult for her or him to find future employment. Even the General discharge has a less-than-satisfactory connotation, provides few benefits, and will look suspect to prospective employers.

When I returned to Lawrence (to my children's delight), I told them I would probably be active in gay organizations and since more people would know about me, they might hear about my lesbianism. I'd be sorry if anyone said something bad, but I wanted my daughters to know they could share that with me and come to me for support. The risk that my kids will get hurt or be hassled is the only thing I regret about being out. They don't deserve any of that (of course *we* don't, either) and it's not fair, like any kind of prejudice against any minority.

Unfortunately, they have experienced two or three incidents of overt discrimination and I've hurt for and with them through these times. Last year I took them to see a wonderful movie about lesbian mothers, "In the Best Interests of the Children." They told some girlfriends about the movie, the friends told their parents, and the parents freaked out. All of a sudden their kids couldn't be around me, although I'd been friendly with them for years, and of *course* they could no longer spend the night with my girls. Those restrictions were somewhat modified after I spoke with the parents, but it is still hard for my kids to understand why people can feel that way and react so negatively.

Then at the beginning of this school year my older girl, Jackie, got a lot of flak about me from other seventh graders and she was labeled a lesbian herself. Naturally this was pretty disturbing to her but we talked it out. We concluded that reacting to her tormentors would only incite them to further harassment, so she decided to ignore them. They have since let up and many other kids have come to her support. I was especially concerned here because junior high itself can be an overwhelming and tough experience without something like this happening.

On the other hand, some benefits have come from both their struggles and mine: my daughters are very tolerant and accepting of all kinds of people; they are very much their own persons, and they have courage and independence and a real sense of the meaning of human rights. They respect others' differences (including their classmates) and they often react with indignation to reports of discrimination against minority groups.

For a long time now I've been very glad that my kids are women-children. I don't think I would love a son less, but it is so much easier to relate to my kids because they are female and thus it is easier to share a really honest, open, caring relationship with them. They know they can discuss anything they want to with me, and I hope we will continue to share such open communication.

I'm often asked if I want my daughters to be gay, also. My reply is that I wish for them to be happy, fulfilled, loving and well-loved women, just as they are now as children. If they are gay, OK; if they are straight or bisexual, that's OK, too. It will be their choice and I don't care to influence that, anymore than I may do, unintentionally. They know I feel this way. In fact, my oldest is currently as boy-crazy as the rest of her friends and she shares these feelings freely with me.

I cherish my daughters' words of acceptance. For example, one day last summer while I was strolling hand-in-hand with my younger girl, Jennie, she just popped out with, "Mom, I love you!" Me: "I love you, too!" And then curiously, I asked her, "Why do you love me, Hon?" "Because you're just *you*, and you *like* it." Wonderful!

And when I asked Jackie if she'd like to contribute to this piece, she wrote:

> "Having a gay Mom is not really as terrible as a lot of people think. Some of my friends think it's cool and say it's different but it's not something to put down (which is true). But

unfortunately a lot of people think it is. Having a gay relative is sometimes special though. People look up to you because you have someone who's different. Frequently you get labeled gay yourself because your Mom is which happens to me a lot. I don't think my Mom is stupid or out of her mind because she decided to be gay. I think she decided to be what *she* wanted to be, not what other people said she should be."

There's not much I can add except to say that my greatest wish for my daughters is to know a world more tolerant and understanding than ours—one which will accept, honor and value them, *whoever* they may be.

DPAT MATTIE

No Name He Can Say

i hate telephone. they make noise, jangle nerves, destroy moments, and seldom bring worthwhile news. i love letters—to write to receive written words usually translatable to i am thinking of you i miss you i want to share this with you. words to savor again words to caress with eye sound with voice hear with heart. phone words bullets to a target.

a folder on my desk is labelled "letters to mark," in parentheses i have written "letters from mark." the folder contains 2 letters in the "to mark" category. they are long painful letters written to explain the choices i had to make to keep living—choices when he was fifteen to "give him away" to his father. it was my time to come out. it had taken me 35 years to be ready. and i thought that this male child whom i so loved and who so loved me was in my way. some things can never be explained no matter how many letters. there have been no letters from mark. perhaps, i tell myself, he does not like to write he is too busy he will when he has something to say he never will.

20 years and one week separate us in age. in the years since our first introduction—a red-faced furry lusty bloody baby laid upon the stomach of a tired frightened new mother—has come and gone a closeness. now more than time and space between us.

October 7, 1976. i am soon to be 39. the telephone rings cutting through the solitude of a poem in process. the right words had been at the tip of my pen. they are gone. he asks my lover if i am home. he uses my old married name. the name i carried for 20 years. one i stopped using 2 years ago. he knows that. she says that dpat is home. he asks for the other name. i have not seen him since may 1974. i have not heard his voice for a year. it is deep. he sounds like his father. he has a prodding confident demanding male voice. it does not fit my image of him. i am overjoyed and i tell him. he says "i don't know what to call you."

"HEY, MOM! CAN I CALL YOU PAT?" HE IS SMILING. AT SIX HE AWAITS THE RETURN OF FOUR FRONT TEETH. THE NEW CREW CUT MAKES HIS EYES LOOK WIDER HIS EARS

BIGGER. HE HAS BEEN RIDING HIS BIKE IN THE SUMMER
HEAT AND HE SMELLS LIKE A SWEATY LITTLE BOY. HE
HUGS ME AND OUR SKINS STICK TOGETHER. WE LAUGH.
I JUST HAD A SHOWER. NOW I SMELL LIKE A LITTLE BOY.
"CAN I, MOM?" "WELL, I GUESS SO. BUT WHY?" "JIM CALLS
HIS MOM CONNIE." "O.K." GRABBING A BROWNIE FROM
THE COOKIE TIN HE RUNS OUT, THE DOOR BANGING BE-
HIND HIM. "SEE YOU LATER, PAT. BYE, MOM!"
   "i don't know what to call you now. mom doesn't feel good
anymore. i don't know dpat. why did you change your name?
. . . i wrote you a really long letter but i didn't mail it because
i was so angry and i said things like 'don't you think you're a
little queer?' ha! ha! pardon the pun."
   "MOM, WHAT'S A QUEER?" I CHOOSE WORDS CARE-
FULLY FOR A SEVEN YEAR OLD. (HE MUST NEVER KNOW
ABOUT ME. NO ONE MUST EVER KNOW ABOUT ME, OR
THEY'LL TAKE HIM AWAY.) "THAT'S A SLANG WORD FOR
A PERSON WHO LOVES ANOTHER PERSON OF THE SAME
SEX—A MAN A MAN, A WOMAN A WOMAN." "UGH!"
"WHAT'S UGH ABOUT LOVE?" "DO YOU THINK IT'S O.K.,
MOM?" "OF COURSE I DO." (BUT I DIDN'T. NOT THEN.)
"THE RIGHT WORD IS HOMOSEXUAL NOT QUEER." HIS
FATHER OVERHEARS THIS DISCUSSION AND SAYS HE
THINKS THEY'RE ALL SICK.
   "you'll never believe what's happened to me," he says, "last
february 19, 1976, i found the lord." i stifled the urge to ask
him if the lord had been lost. "you won't believe the difference
it has made in my life. now i go to church all day sunday and
twice during the week. i always read my Bible and i spend a
lot of time witnessing to others about what jesus has done for
me. i love to get ahold of holier than thou catholics and mealy
mouthed christians." my words do not get in edgewise.
   "I WILL NOT! I DON'T WANT TO GO BACK THERE TO
THAT OLD CHURCH. ALL THEY DO IS TALK ABOUT JESUS
JESUS JESUS AND GOD GOD GOD. NONE OF IT'S TRUE ANY-
WAY. YOU CAN'T MAKE ME GO." AT EIGHT ALREADY
MAKING UP HIS MIND ABOUT WHAT HE NEEDED. HIS RELI-
GION A WALK IN THE WOODS AND HIS DOG.
   half an hour of sermonizing and then the questions. "how do
you justify your, well, your homosexuality?" "i don't have to

justify it to you or to anyone else." "well, the bible says" and
there are quotes. "how do you square all this with god? what
would jesus think? don't you want to be saved?" that's what
the red faced men scream at me down at the powell street cable
car turnaround, clutching their black new testaments like cleav-
ers, chopping the air with invective and spittle. a verse begins
to weave around and around through the conversation. i do not
catch the citation but christ is saying that he has no mother.

i have gotten mark's message but he does not hear mine. i want
to hang up and don't. "and you lied in that poem. i never said it
was alright. you lied!" (he is talking about the title poem of a
poetry collection i have published—*no lies, no more, not now*.)
WE SAT IN THE HAMBURGER PLACE EATING PEANUTS
AND TALKING. I TOLD HIM OF MY LESBIANISM AND THAT
I WAS LEAVING FOR CALIFORNIA WITH THE WOMAN I
LIVED WITH. SHE WAS WITH US. HE LOOKED AT US AND
SAID "IT'S O.K., MOM. I DON'T UNDERSTAND HOW OR WHY
ANYONE LOVES ANYONE ELSE." AND WE SAT AND
TALKED OF LOVE. WE DROVE HIM HOME. I WALKED HIM
TO THE APARTMENT DOOR, SAID GOODBYE AND STARTED
TO HUG HIM. HE PULLED AWAY. THAT WAS THE LAST
TIME I SAW HIM.

"i didn't say those things." i can visualize him on his knees
praying to his angry god.

"i don't know what i think of you," he says.

"HEY, MOM, MOM!" THE VOICE IS IN THE NEXT AISLE.
AISLE 6 MAYONNAISE JELLY COFFEE TEA. I AM SELECTING
CEREAL. HE ROUNDS THE CORNER ON A RUN CRASHING
INTO A CART. HE PICKS HIMSELF OFF THE FLOOR RUNS
TO ME THROWS HIS ARMS AROUND ME. "I LOVE YOU,
MOM." HE IS 9.

"guess i ought to wish you happy birthday." i thank him and
start to tell him what my lover and i will do to celebrate. he
changes the subject. he starts to talk about "screwing" some
young women. he keeps using the term "my manhood."
THE STREET IS WET FROM DAYS OF RAIN. I AIM THE
BIKE AT THE USUAL SPOT ON THE CURB WHERE I CUT
ACROSS AND THE TIRE SLIPS. THE DOCTOR SAYS I WILL
HAVE TO USE THE CRUTCHES FOR 6 WEEKS. IT IS A WEEK
BEFORE MY THIRTY-FOURTH BIRTHDAY. "HEY, MOM, CAN

YOU STOP BY THE BAKERY ON YOUR WAY HOME FROM SCHOOL? I ORDERED SOME OF THOSE REAL GOOD DOUBLE CHOCOLATE CUPCAKES BUT I WON'T HAVE TIME TO PICK THEM UP BEFORE YOU GET HOME." THE BAKERY BOX IS BIG AND HE SETS IT IN THE MIDDLE OF THE TABLE. THERE ARE FIVE PACKAGES AROUND THE BOX. "GO AHEAD, MOM, YOU OPEN THE CUPCAKES." THE CAKE IS HUGE. IT IS MY FAVORITE—CHOCOLATE WITH CHOCOLATE ICING. ON TOP IT SAYS "HAPPY BIRTHDAY ANCIENT CRIPPLE." THE CARD IS A PICTURE OF A GREEN TURTLE IN A GREEN SHELL. INSIDE HE HAS WRITTEN: "ANOTHER WRINKLE ON YOUR SHELL? SO WHAT THE HELL. YOU'RE NOT GETTING OLDER YOU'RE GETTING MORE BEAUTIFUL. LOVE, YOUR SON MARK." HE IS 13.

"you know giving me to my dad was the best thing you ever did. sure glad i didn't have to live with you."

HE IS STANDING BY THE STOVE MAKING HIMSELF SOME HOT CHOCOLATE. TOMORROW HE GOES TO LIVE WITH HIS FATHER. THEY DO NOT LIKE EACH OTHER. HE IS 15. AND 6 FEET TALL. "I FEEL LIKE I'M GOING TO SUMMER CAMP. ONLY I KNOW I'LL NEVER COME HOME AGAIN." SOBBING HE RUNS INTO HIS ROOM.

he finally says well maybe he'll come out to visit me at christmas. he does not acknowledge the other person in my life. this news is followed by more biblical quotes. he says goodbye. so do i. he has not called me mom or pat or dpat. he has without using the words been calling me sinner, queer, lost and damned. the next day I write a letter taking 5 pages to say "if you are coming to see me dpat mattie lesbian mother because you want to see me please come quickly and stay as long as you like. if on the other hand you are coming with thoughts of attempted conversions stay where you are. i have witnessed personally and through other people's experiences the pain and destruction of life and hope that has resulted from pious bible thumping bigots. i fight that behavior every way i can." there has been no reply.

It is the price i chose to pay for me, my sanity and my freedom. he does not understand and my words make little difference. i have his pictures arranged before me on this sunday afternoon. a chubby laughing baby, a 3-year-old's thrilled christmas morning, a 5-year-old's hot day at the beach, an awkward gangly cracked voiced teenager, a young man i hardly recognize in the graduation gown. he is beautiful. he is probably in church. maybe praying for his sinful mother who has no name he can say.

DEL MARTIN & PHYLLIS LYON

Anniversary

Since Gay couplings are not recognized by religion, the law or society-at-large, our silver or golden anniversaries are usually celebrated "in the closet" and go unnoted in the society section of the local newspaper. The occasion of our 25th anniversary, however, proved to be an exception. As a matter of fact—and much to our surprise—it became a *cause célèbre* in San Francisco.

Del is a native San Franciscan and was salutatorian of the first graduating class at George Washington High School. Phyllis, though born in Tulsa, Oklahoma, was reared in the Bay Area and graduated from the University of California at Berkeley. We are both long-time activists in the Democratic Party and in both the Gay and Women's Movements. Thus many people—both heterosexual and homosexual—have touched and influenced our lives, and we wanted to share our anniversary celebration with those who were still in the area.

Because there were so many of them and because our home is so small, we decided to hold a two-day weekend "open house." We got a crew of women to help and sent out several hundred invitations. The only thing we had to worry about, we thought, was the possibility that everyone might arrive on the same day and at the same hour—which would have been disastrous.

In the midst of our preparations—trying to run down friends who had moved or with whom we had lost touch—we were suddenly besieged by the news media. As a surprise for us, Supervisor Carol Ruth Silver had requested the Board of Supervisors to issue an official Certificate of Honor "in appreciative public recognition of distinction and merit, to Del Martin and Phyllis Lyon on the occasion of their Twenty-Fifth Anniversary and for their years of devoted service to San Francisco." The surprise, as it turned out, was on Supervisor Silver. Ordinarily such certificates are routinely approved by the Board without comment, but in this instance—an honor for a lesbian couple—there was a 50-minute debate.

"Twenty-five years of what?" shouted one supervisor. Another claimed that some citizens had moral reservations about such relationships and that the Board "shouldn't rub their noses in it." Several supervisors, whom we count among our personal friends, rose to our defense and expressed outrage at these comments. And the first speaker declared he could sum up his feelings in just four words: "Toleration, yes—glorification, no!" Another supervisor then moved to separate the question: recognition of our service to the community from recognition of our anniversary. The motion failed. And finally, on a vote of 8 to 2 we were awarded the certificate of honor as originally presented.

The controversy, of course, prompted the publicity that the dissenters had wished to avoid. It gave the Gay community the opportunity to observe just who our political friends are and the vehicle by which to educate the public by showing that Gay relationships, myths to the contrary, are often stable and long-lasting. A private celebration of our "silver" anniversary, which would otherwise have gone unnoticed except for our friends, became a public affair. With cameras flashing and much fanfare, Supervisors Silver, Ella Hill Hutch and Harvey Milk (the city's first elected Gay official) presented us the certificate. The event was favorably reported in both of the city's daily newspapers, on television and radio, and even in a New York magazine.

Over the two days of the weekend preceding Valentine's Day 1978 (the actual date of our anniversary) some 400 friends descended upon our home, which we lovingly call Habromania Haven. Habromania is defined as a state of consciousness "characterized by delusions of a pleasing nature." Despite the challenges of American society which has been historically homophobic, we have a relationship—between ourselves personally and with many San Franciscans—that has been most rewarding and certainly of a "pleasing nature."

Back in 1953 when we first made a commitment to each other the atmosphere in San Francisco, so far as Gays were concerned, was anything but pleasant. Then we were deep in the closet and lived in constant fear that we would be exposed, fired from our jobs or thrown in jail just for being "different." While it is true that we opened a joint bank account early on, the names of depositors were not printed on the checks as they are now.

Our "coming out" was an evolutionary process in which we gradually took more and more calculated risks—risks that eventually paid off. It began in 1955 with the founding of the Daughters of Bilitis, a Lesbian social club. DOB gave us the opportunity to meet other women like ourselves outside of the Gay bars, which were then subject to intermittent police raids. We began by meeting in our homes where we felt safe, but later became a California-chartered non-profit organization, rented a downtown office, published a magazine, held public meetings and established chapters in other large cities across the country.

Efforts of DOB and the Mattachine Society, a Gay male organization, to become public were largely ignored in the 50s by what we called a "conspiracy of silence" on the part of the media. A turning point was the 1959 municipal election in which the incumbent mayor was accused of "harboring homosexuals" because two Gay organizations maintained their national headquarters in San Francisco. Members of both groups, instead of stampeding back into the closet, stood their ground and became even more determined to establish civil rights for Gay citizens. The next year the Daughters of Bilitis held the first national Lesbian convention, an event that was not only covered by the press, but also by the "homosexual detail" of the San Francisco Police Department.

By the mid-60s DOB and Mattachine had been joined by such organizations as the Tavern Guild, an association of Gay bar owners and employees who had banded together for mutual protection; the Council on Religion and the Homosexual, which began a dialogue with the Church; the Society for Individual Rights, which established the city's first Gay Center; and Citizens Alert, a coalition of ethnic minorities and Gays to deal with police harassment and brutality.

The 70s brought many more changes: establishment of Gay foundations, business associations, political organizations, and the Metropolitan Community Church. With these came Gay caucuses within professional associations, addition of Gays as a protected class under the city ordinance that established the Human Rights Commision, appointment of Lesbians and Gay men to city commissions and task forces, and election of the first Gay to the San Francisco Board of Supervisors. Lesbian involvement in the feminist movement working for women's issues helped to gain the support of heterosexual women for Gay rights, and in turn to get Gay men to understand their need to support women's rights.

We saw our anniversary as a means of bringing together many of the people who had helped to bring us from the isolation and fear of the 50s to a real sense of "belonging" in the 70s. We must also admit we hoped to pay some of our social debts, since activism, we have found, often interferes with our social life. The joy we felt as we greeted old friends and new is difficult to express. We literally glowed when we saw some of the early DOB members chatting with a judge or commissioner, when a Gay male couple of 30 years standing mingled with heterosexual couples, when Gay and straight persons of color acknowledged each other socially, when the mayor phoned and offered his congratulations, when a state senator and his wife expressed gratitude for our friendship.

"The integration of the homosexual into society" had been an early—and seemingly impossible—goal of the Daughters of Bilitis. We are proud to have played a role in making the impossible possible.

MONIKA KEHOE

An Incident in the Fifties

As I marched in the Gay Pride Parade in San Francisco in the summer of 1978, I couldn't help thinking how far we have come since that time, a quarter of a century earlier, when I faced a federal investigation of my life style simply to be able to continue in U.S. Civil Service. I was then a GS-14 and eligible for promotion to GS-15, the highest rank not requiring Congressional approval. I had served earlier for a number of years as a civil servant in administrative posts overseas and, although I was currently teaching in a private university, I was, of course, interested in returning to government work in order to complete the few years necessary to qualify for the quite substantial federal pension involved. I was forty-three years old, and a full professor with a Ph.D. I had more than two decades of experience in national and international government service including a top post in the UN Secretariat for several years. I was single and had no dependents—an ideal employee, it seemed, for assignments abroad.

But now, quite suddenly, in the winter of 1954, I was summoned to an "interview" in the Federal Building in New York City. The letter from the U.S. Civil Service Commission gave no hint of its purpose. When I entered the room on my arrival, however, I had an ominous feeling that this was not to be just another job evaluation or work-related discussion.

For the first three days of the ordeal, the five men sitting behind the long table were scrupulously polite. One of them took my coat each day when I came in and helped me on with it when I left. None ever failed to address me as "Dr. Kehoe" and, when I entered the interrogation room, the men always stood until after I was seated.

The fourth day, however, turned out to be a little different. I was escorted, not to the usual chair in front of the long table, but to a smaller room nearby, where the expressionless female stenotypist was already installed. A young man with red hair, whom I had not seen before, smiled a welcome greeting. He didn't take my coat, which I hung on the back of a chair. Instead, he asked me to sit down near a desk where he carefully placed a folder. I could see my name along the spine. I wondered what was scheduled for today and what had happened to my panel of inquisitors. Had they tired of their attempts to pin the communist label on me? Had I finally convinced them that I was really apolitical? They knew I had never voted—perhaps in their minds that showed a lack of patriotism, even though I explained that I had never been any place at the proper time to register. Or had they exhausted all the incriminating information they had so assiduously gathered about me? Like my dancing with the USSR liaison officer in Seoul? Or my application to the U.S. embassy to visit the University of Pyonyang, North Korea? Or my earlier subscription to that wrongly opinionated journal, *The New Republic*? Or maybe the fact that I had read the "Communist Manifesto" in school? Or the more devastating fact that I had not asked for the return of my body to U.S. soil in case I died out of the country? Or even the neighborhood tenants' gathering I had attended when I lived in the Village years before—the one that the landlords had called a commie protest meeting—when all we were concerned with was getting the garbage cleaned up in the alley so we could control the rats in our apartments? At any rate I could sense that today's inquiry was about to take a new turn. The first question posed by the redhead gave me my clue. "Are you a homosexual?"

Even though the query was spoken in an almost embarrassed voice, it carried quite a bit of clout in the McCarthy-rife atmosphere of the time.

The pause before I replied was probably fraught with guilt, at least to the ear of my interviewer. I watched the typist's fingers hover above her keys waiting for my answer while she chewed her gum with abandon.

"What do you mean by *homosexual*?" I was obviously playing for time.

"You ought to know, if you are one," he said flatly, with some emphasis on the *you* and *are*.

"But I can't answer a question I don't understand," I parried.

"Well, do you prefer women to men?"

"As a rule, don't you?" Now I was getting smart-alecky and I reminded myself that this was no place to be cute.

"You know very well what I mean." His face was getting red like his hair as he got more specific. "Do you prefer sleeping with women?"

"I prefer sleeping alone," I replied. "Any bed-partner keeps me awake."

"You have lived with different women," he went on with a sneer in his voice, "according to your record. You even managed to take one of your friends overseas with you on a civil service appointment." He was reading now from a yellow sheet of paper clipped in my file. "And, on another Far East tour, you lived at the home of one of your Asian women friends, rather than in your assigned billet."

"Yes, military housing in Tokyo left something to be desired. It was particularly uncomfortable—even unsafe—with all the drunken officers about." I tried to look indignant.

"When you lived in the Village in New York City, you frequented lesbian bars on both the Lower East Side and the Village. Your name appears on two of the raid lists made by the vice squad.

"Is that an indictment? What about all the tourists' names that were also on those lists? Were they all homosexuals?" I remembered how worried I had been at the time. I was Dean of Women at one of New York's more respectable colleges and had been taking an awful chance in order to satisfy my curiosity about what was then called the demimonde.

"Please answer the question," the redhead sputtered.

"You didn't ask a question," I pointed out.

"Dr. Kehoe, this is a very unsatisfactory conversation and I believe nothing is to be gained by continuing it."

I couldn't have agreed more. What a patsy he was! Probably a frequenter of far worse places than I had ever heard of. These uptight, buttoned-down defenders of the public morals were amusing at best.

As he rose from his chair, he closed my bulky dossier. "That is all; we'll be in touch with you by letter in a few days." I put on my coat and left, wondering what would happen next—another invitation, perhaps? This time to appear in Washington under the baton of McCarthy himself? I was genuinely apprehensive. Important people had been pilloried right and left. Their careers and lives destroyed. Maybe the government vice squad was getting down to the small fry. Nobody knew how far this witch hunt would go.

That same day, I returned to Boston where I was teaching and, sure enough, the next week brought a notice from the Civil Service Commission that, as a result of the "Federal Hearing," I would be barred from employment by the U.S. government for two years for "security reasons." Of course, this was simply a euphemism for what was officially known as moral turpitude. Since I was in a private university at the time, and quite happy, being ostracized from civil service was not as bad a punishment for my "moral turpitude" as it might have been at another time of my life. I breathed a sigh of relief and dropped the notice in the wastebasket beside my desk.

I have sometimes thought since that I should have been angry or at least indignant at the affront of the whole affair, but I guess I was aware of the prevailing Zeitgeist and had nothing but contempt for it. My only concern was to keep a low profile and not jeopardize my job. Certainly I never had any intention of altering my life style or changing my wayward ways. And I never have.

AUDRE LORDE

Of Sisters and Secrets*

When I was little, around the age of four or five, I would have given anything I had in the world except my mother, in order to have had a friend or a little sister. She would be someone I could talk to and play with, someone close enough in age to me that I would not have to be afraid of her, nor she of me. We would share our secrets with each other.

Even though I had two older sisters, I grew up feeling like an only child, since they were quite close to each other in age and quite far away from me. Actually, I grew up feeling like an only planet, or some isolated world in a hostile, or at best, unfriendly, firmament. The fact that I was clothed, sheltered and fed better than many other children in Harlem in those Depression years was not a fact that impressed itself too often upon my child's consciousness.

Most of my childhood fantasies revolved around how I might acquire this little female person for my companion. I concentrated upon magical means, having gathered early on that my family had no intention of satisfying this particular need of mine. The Lorde family was not going to expand any more.

The idea of having children was a pretty scary one, anyway, full of secret indiscretions peeked at darkly through the corner of an eye, as my mother and my aunts did whenever they passed a woman on the street who had one of those big, pushed-out-in-front, flowered blouses that always intrigued me so. I longed just once to get close enough to peer up under the pretty cloth and see exactly what secret was hidden up there. I always wondered what great wrong these women had done, that this big blouse was a badge of, obvious as the dunce-cap I sometimes had to wear in the corner at school.

Adoption was also out of the question. You could get a kitten from the corner grocery store man, but not a sister. Like ocean cruises and boarding schools and upper berths in trains, it was not for us. Rich people, like Mr. Rochester in *Jane Eyre*, lonely

*From "Prosepiece."

in their great tree-lined estates, adopted children, but not the Lordes.

Being the youngest in a West Indian family had many privileges but no rights. And since my mother was determined not to 'spoil' me, even those privileges were largely illusory. I knew, therefore, that if my family were to acquire another little person voluntarily, that little person would most probably be a boy, and would most decidedly belong to my mother, and not to me.

I really believed, however, that my magical endeavors, done often enough, in the right way, and in the right places, letter-perfect and with a clean soul, would finally bring me a little sister. And I did mean little. I frequently imagined my little sister and I having fascinating conversations together while she sat cradled in the cupped palm of my hand. There she was, curled up and carefully shielded from the inquisitive eyes of the rest of the world and my family in particular.

When I was four I got my first eyeglasses, and I stopped tripping over my feet all the time. I still walked with my head down, though, all the time, counting the lines of the squares in the pavement of every street which I traveled, hanging onto the hand of my mother or one of my sisters. I had decided that if I could step on all the horizontal lines for five days, my little person would appear like a dream made real, waiting for me in my bed by the time I got home. But I always messed up, or skipped one, or someone pulled my arm at a crucial moment. And she never appeared.

I didn't even really have a bed for her to appear in, anyway, since I slept in my parents' bedroom on a cot that was folded neatly away during the day.

Sometimes on Saturdays in winter, my mother made the three of us a little clay out of flour and water and Diamond Crystal Shaker Salt, and I always fashioned tiny little figures out of my share of the mixture. I would beg or swipe a little vanilla extract off my mother's shelf in the kitchen where she kept her wonderful spices and herbs and extracts, and mix that with the clay. Sometimes I dabbed the figures on either side of the head behind the ears as I had seen my mother do with her glycerine and rosewater whenever she got dressed to go out.

I loved the way the rich, dark brown vanilla scented the flour-clay; it reminded me of my mother's hands when she made peanut brittle and eggnog at holidays. But most of all, I loved the live color it would bring to the pasty-white clay.

I knew for sure that real live people came in many different shades of beige and brown and cream and reddish tan, but nobody alive ever came in that pasty white shade of flour and salt and water, even if they were called white. So the vanilla was essential if my little person was to be real. But the coloring didn't help either.

No matter how many intricate rituals and incantations and spells I performed, no matter how many Hail Marys and Our Fathers I said, no matter what I promised god in return, the vanilla-tinted clay would slowly shrivel up and harden, turning gradually brittle and sour, and then crumbling into a grainy flour dust. No matter how hard I prayed or schemed, the figures would never come alive. They never turned around in the cupped palm of my hand, to smile up at me and say "Hi."

My sisters and I never got along very well together. To me until this day, the essence of sorrow and sadness, like a Picasso painting still-lifed and forever living, is the forlorn and remembered sight of a discarded silk stocking brick-caught and hanging against the rain-windy side of a tenement building wall opposite our kitchen window from which I hung, suspended by one hand, and screaming at my elder sister who had been left in charge of the three of us while my mother went out marketing.

What our interactions had been before is lost to me now, but my mother came home just in time to pull me back inside the dark kitchen, saving me from a one-story drop into the air shaft below. I don't remember the terror and fury I must have felt, but I remember the whipping that both my sister and I got. More than that I remember the sadness and the deprivation and the loneliness of that discarded, torn, and brick-caught silk stocking, broken and hanging against the wall in the tenement rain.

I was always very jealous of my two older sisters, because they were older and therefore more privileged, and because they had each other for a friend. They could talk to one another without censure or punishment, or so I thought.

As far as I was concerned, Phyllis and Helen led a magical and charmed existence down the hall in their room. It was tiny but complete, with privacy and a place to be away from the eternal parental eye which was my lot, sleeping as I did in

my parents' bedroom and having only the public parts of the
house to play in. I was never alone, nor far from my mother's
watchful eye. The bathroom door was the only door in the house
that I was ever allowed to close behind me, and even that would
be opened with an inquiry if I tarried too long on the toilet.

The first time I ever slept anywhere else besides in my parents'
bedroom was a milestone in my journey to this house of myself.
When I was four and five, my family went to the Connecticut
shore for a week's vacation during the summer. This was much
grander than a day's outing to Rockaway Beach or Coney Island,
and much more exciting.

First of all, we got to sleep in a house that was not ours, and
Daddy was with us during the day. Then there were strange
new foods to sample, like blue soft-shelled crab, which my
father ordered for his lunch and would sometimes persuade my
mother to let me have a taste of. We children were not allowed
such alien and suspected fare, but on Fridays we did have fried
shrimp and little batter cakes with pieces of clam in them. They
were good, and very different from my mother's codfish-and-
potato fishcakes which were our favorite Friday dinner back
home.

The first year we were there I slept on a cot in my parents'
room just as at home, and I always went to bed early. Just as
at home, the watery colors of twilight would come in to terrify
me, shining greenly through the buff-colored window-shades,
high up on the windows like blind eyes near my bed. I hated
the twilight color and going to bed before anyone else, far from
the comfortingly familiar voices of my mother and father on
the porch of this rooming house which belonged to my father's
real estate buddy who was giving us a good deal for the week.

Those yellow-green window-shade twilights were the color
of loneliness for me, and that has never left me. Everything else
about that first summer week in Connecticut is lost to me, except
the two photographs which show me, as usual, discontent and
squinting up against the sun.

The second year we were even poorer, or maybe my father's
real estate friend had raised his prices. For whatever reason,
the five of us shared one room, and there was no space for an
extra cot. The room had three windows in it, and two double
beds that sagged ever so slightly in the middle of their white

chenille-spread-covered expanses. My sisters and I shared one
of these beds.

I was still put to bed earlier than my sisters, who were allowed
to stay up and listen to "I Love A Mystery" on the old upright
cabinet radio that sat in the living room downstairs near the
porch window. Its soft tones would drift out across the porch
to the cretonne-covered rocking chairs lined up in a row in the
soft-salty back-street shore-resort night.

I didn't mind the twilights so much that year. We had a back
room and it got dark earlier, so it was always night by the time
I went to bed. Unterrified by the twilight green, I had no trouble
at all falling asleep.

My mother supervised the brushing of my teeth, and the saying of my prayers, and then after assuring herself that all was
in order, she kissed me goodnight, and turned out the light of
the dim, unshaded bulb.

The door closed. I lay awake, rigid with excitement, waiting
for "I Love A Mystery" to be over, and for my sisters to come
and get into bed beside me. I made bargains with god to keep
me awake. I bit my lips and pinched the soft fleshy parts of
my palms with my fingernails, all to keep myself from falling
asleep.

After an eternity of 30 minutes, during which I reviewed the
entire contents of my day including what I should and shouldn't
have done that I didn't or did do, I heard my sisters' footsteps
in the hallway. The door to our room opened and they stepped
into the darkness.

"Hey, Audre. You still wake?" That was Helen, four years
older than I and the closest to me in age.

I was torn with indecision. What should I do? If I didn't
answer, she might tickle my toes, and if I did answer, what
should I say?

"Say, are you wake?"

"No," I whispered in a squeaky little voice I thought consistent
with a sleeping state.

"Sure enough, see, she still wake." I heard Helen's disgusted
whisper to Phyllis, followed by the sharp intake of her breath
as she sucked her teeth. "Look her eyes wide open still."

The bed creaked on one side of me. "What you still doin' up,
like a ninny? On the way in, you know, I tell the boogieman

come bite your head off, and he comin' just now to get you good."

"I felt the bed sag under the weight of both of their bodies, one on either side of me. My mother had decreed that I should sleep in the middle, to keep me from falling out of bed, as well as to separate my two sisters. I was so enchanted with the idea of sharing a bed with them that I couldn't have cared less. Helen reached over and gave me a little preliminary pinch.

"Ouch!" I rubbed my tender upper arm, now sore from her strong little piano-trained fingers. "Oh I goin' to tell Mommy how you pinching me and you goin' to get a whipping sure enough." And then, triumphantly, I played my hole card. "And to besides, I goin' to tell her too what among-you do in bed every night!"

"Go ahead, ninny, run your mouth. You goin' to run it once too often til it drop off your face and then just see where it's goin' to get you." Helen sucked her teeth again, but moved her hand away.

"Oh, just go to sleep now, Audre." That was Phyllis, my older sister, who was always the peacemaker, the placid, reasonable one. But I knew perfectly well what I had pinched my palms to stay awake for, and I was waiting, barely able to contain myself.

For that summer, in that hot back room of a resort slum, I had finally found out what my sisters did at home at night in that little room which they shared across from the bathroom at the end of the hall, that enticing little room which I was never allowed to enter except by an invitation that never came.

They told each other stories. They told each other stories in endless installments, making up the episodes as they went along, from the fantasies engendered by the radio adventure shows which we were all addicted to listening to in those days.

There was "Buck Rogers," and "I Love A Mystery," "Jack Armstrong, All-American Boy," "The Green Hornet," and "Quiet Please." There was "The FBI In Peace And War," "Mr. District Attorney," "The Lone Ranger," and my all-time favorite, "The Shadow," whose power to cloud men's minds so they could not see him was something I did not stop lusting for until quite recently.

I thought that the very idea of telling stories and not getting whipped for telling untrue was the most marvelous thing I could think of that year, and every night that week I begged to be allowed to listen, not realizing that they couldn't stop. Phyllis didn't mind so long as I kept my mouth shut, but by bedtime Helen had had enough of her pesky little sister and my endless stream of questions. And her stories were always by far and away the best, filled with tough little girls who masqueraded in boys' clothing and always foiled the criminals, managing to save the day.

"Please, Phyllis?" I wheedled. There was a long moment of quiet, with Helen sucking her teeth ominously, then Phyllis, whispering,

"All right. Who turn it is tonight?"

"I not saying a word 'till she asleep!" That was Helen, determined.

"Please Phyllis, please let me listen?"

"No! No such thing!" Helen was adamant.

"Please, Phyllis, I promise I be quiet." I could feel Helen swelling up beside me like a bullfrog, but I persisted, not realizing or not caring that my appeal to Phyllis's authority as the elder sister only infuriated Helen even more.

Phyllis was not only softhearted, but very practical, with the pragmatic approach of an 11-year-old girl.

"Now you promise you never goin' to tell?"

I felt like I was being inducted into the most secret of societies.

"Cross my heart." Catholic girls never hoped to die.

Helen was obviously not convinced. I stifled a squeak as she nipped me again with her fingers, this time on the thigh.

"I getting tired of all this, you know. So if you ever so much as breathe a *word* about my stories, Sandman's comin' after you the very same minute to pluck out you eyes like a mackerel for soup." And Helen smacked her lips suggestively, as she gave way with her parting shot.

I could just see those little rubbery eyeballs swimming about in the bottom of the Friday night fish stew, and I shuddered.

"I promise, Helen, cross my heart. I don't say a word to nobody, and I be so quiet, you'll see." I put both of my hands up across my mouth in the darkness, jittering with anticipation.

It was Helen's turn to begin.

"Where were we, now? Oh yes, so me and Buck had just fetched back the sky-horse when Doc . . ."

I could not resist. Down came my hands.

"No, no, Helen, not yet. Don't you remember? Doc hadn't gotten there yet, because . . ." I didn't want to miss a single thing.

Helen's little brown fingers shot across the bedclothes and gave me such a nip on the buttocks that I screeched in pain. Her voice was high and indignant and full of helpless fury.

"You see that? You see that? What did I tell you, Phyllis?" She was almost wailing in fury. "I knew it! She can't keep that miserable tongue in she mouth a minute. Sure enough, I told you so, didn't I? Didn't I? And now to besides she want to steal me story!"

"Sh-h-h-h! The two o-you! Mommy's comin' back here just now, and among you two goin' to make us all catch hell!"

But Helen wasn't going to play any more. I felt her flop over on her side with her disgruntled back towards me, and then I could feel our bed shaking with her angry sobs of rage, muffled in the sweaty pillow.

I could have kicked myself. "I truly sorry, Helen," I ventured. And I really was, because I realized that my big mouth had done me out of a night's installment, and probably of all the installments for the rest of the week. I also knew that Mother would never let me out of her sight the next day long enough for me to catch up to my sisters, as they ran off down the beach to complete their tale in secret.

"Honest, I didn't mean to, Helen." I tried one last time, reaching over to touch her. But Helen jerked her body sharply backward and her butt caught me in the stomach. I heard her still outraged warning hissed through clenched teeth,

"And don't you dare pat me!" And I had been on the receiving end of her fingers often enough to know when to leave well enough alone.

So I turned over on my stomach, said goodnight to Phyllis, and finally went to sleep, too.

The next morning, I woke up before either Phyllis or Helen. I lay in the middle of the bed, being careful not to touch either one of them. Staring up at the ceiling, I listened to my father snoring, in the next bed, and to the sound of my mother's wedding ring hitting the head-board as in her sleep she flung her arm across her eyes against the morning light. I relished the quiet, the new smells of strange bedclothes and sea-salty air, and the frank beams of yellow sunlight pouring through the high windows like a promise of endless day.

Right then and there, before anybody else woke up, I decided to make up a story of my own.

JUDITH McDANIEL

My Life as the Only Lesbian Professor

I didn't know what to expect. I'd never done it before: moved to a new job and community and announced that I was a lesbian. I knew *why* I was doing it. I could think of no other way to live sanely. For me it was the answer to a black depression that had felt like walking into a tunnel with no light at the end. It was survival: the only way I could imagine facing a new life. I jeopardized no one but myself, I thought I was going alone.

But I didn't know how to do it. I went to my first faculty meetings. I taught my first classes. I assigned *Rubyfruit Jungle*. I wore a ring with a double woman's symbol, but almost no one noticed. A woman who lives with a woman lover is a lesbian; a woman who lives alone is single.

One of my students did notice. She came and sat in my office to talk about George Eliot, but the double woman's symbol *she* wore on a small chain around her neck spoke more eloquently than her words. She came back frequently and brought her friends. We began to speak openly about our lesbianism, about the problems of organizing and running a Women's Coalition on campus.

One afternoon during that first hectic month, two women faculty invited me to have coffee. Except for department functions, it was my first social contact. My students had told me that one of the women was a lesbian, but no one must know; the other, they said, was a feminist with a "closet" boyfriend.

We spoke briefly about our work. "Why did you leave your last job?" They asked. "I was fired," I said, "with another woman. We were too 'feminist.'" "Did you sue them?" one woman asked. "It was difficult," I said. "We were both lesbians."

My comment lay like something unpleasant in the middle of the table. No one referred to it. As our half hour chat ended and we stood to leave, one of the women turned to me and asked angrily, "Just where do you expect to fit into this community?" "I don't know," I responded. And I didn't. It was a question I would ask myself many times.

Not everyone responded with fear. My students asked me to

come to their first Women's Coalition meeting. We were relaxed and shared ideas and experiences. Another young faculty woman was there. She noticed my ring and began to speak enthusiastically about Charlotte Bunch's speech on lesbian feminism at the Socialist Feminist Conference. She wondered, was I interested in a feminist study group? We began to plan for the future.

At a formal dinner for the trustees and faculty, I sat across the table from a faculty wife who told me she was a feminist and—very confidentially—that the reason more students didn't attend Women's Coalition meetings was rumors about LES-BIANS being in control. "Oh," I said, gesturing magnanimously with my wine glass. "That's why I always say I'm a lesbian. It helps other women to know where I'm coming from politically." Her eyes glazed and her wine glass thumped on the table. "Oh really," she said, as her gaze cleared.

In the classroom I was less daring. An audience of one is not as intimidating as thirty. I had worked hard to establish a rapport with my students. At the beginning of the semester I had as-signed *Rubyfruit Jungle* in my Introduction to Fiction course. I was going to use it as an example of the modern picaresque novel. During the first weeks as we struggled through Dickens and Virginia Woolf, I waited anxiously for a comment from someone who might have read the back cover blurb, announcing gaily that *Rubyfruit Jungle* was about "growing up lesbian in America." Not a word from my students. When the time came, I announced that *Rubyfruit Jungle* was due on Monday. I told them about the picaresque novel and Fielding and socially un-acceptable or shocking behavior. And then I quit. I couldn't say the word lesbian in my own classroom. I spent that weekend in a panic. How the hell was I going to teach this book? What could I say about it? Was my own sexual preference relevant to teaching this novel? What would I say if they asked me if I was a lesbian?

By Monday I had resolved nothing. I had spent all weekend preparing a class for which I was totally unprepared. I walked into the classroom, perched casually on the edge of my desk, and asked vaguely, "Well, what did you think of *Rubyfruit Jungle?*" Responses ranged from "best book in the course," "I loved it," "she was so funny," to "weird" and "it was perverted."

Now I had something to deal with; we worked intensely with the book and the students' attitudes for three meetings. At the end of our last scheduled class on the book, a woman raised her hand and hesitantly asked, "Um, can I ask you, um, it may not, um, but . . ." Here it comes, I thought wryly, my moment of truth. "Ask," I said bravely. "Is Rita Mae Brown a *lesbian*?" "Yes," I answered laughing, dismissing the class. "Yes, for sure she is."

Three years later, after many such encounters, I have begun to understand those feelings of fear and insecurity which I experienced in first teaching a lesbian work. The students I teach have been raised in a society that fears and hates homosexuals. When my students did not know I was a lesbian, and when the material we were dealing with made homosexuality a topic of discussion or reference, I was in an extremely vulnerable position. In talking about *Rubyfruit Jungle*, my students—assuming they were among a peer-heterosexual group—could easily have said things that were threatening and hostile to me.

I do my best teaching when I can assume that all of the students in my class know I am a lesbian. Whatever the particular focus of the literature we are discussing, I encourage students to bring their own experiences to that of the literature and to relate literature to their own lives. I need to be able to do the same and my sexual preference is one important part of my identity and experience. When I introduced a course on the poetry of Adrienne Rich, it seemed most natural in talking about her journey from daughter-in-law to lesbian feminist for me to identify with that process. When I teach Christina Rossetti's "Goblin Market," I need to speak unselfconsciously of her use of lesbian imagery, explicitly *sexual* lesbian imagery, growing out of a life that was essentially asexual and reclusive. I cannot be unselfconscious if I need to be on guard, concentrated on defending myself against random attacks.

Within my wider social community, I gradually became identified as a lesbian—a free spirit, as it were. I had hoped I would find a lover in my new community. I had expected I would. I did not expect—and I did not understand until much later—that I was a hot sexual prospect: I was a new dyke in town.

I did have what I called "Rule Number One." Teachers do not become involved with students. It seemed a clear statement of intention to me at the time, that should, I thought, make relationships with my lesbian students open, aboveboard and simple. I believed if I stated my understanding of the contract between us, that would be sufficient. From the very beginning of my contact with students in my new job, I made rule number one an open subject of discussion.

Students seemed to think rule number one was funny. It usually came up in those conversations about male professors who had affairs with their female students. We all had opinions about such things. Mine was that power in such relationships was unequal, and I presumed therefore that the relationship was exploitive; hence rule number one, which I have never broken, I explained. Laughter. Insistence on exceptional relationships. Tension.

By the end of the first semester I had found a new lover, not in my own community, but within commuting distance. I had not told many women about her. When she moved in with me, I did not consider it a community project. My love life was my own, I thought. A student confided in me later that when my lover had appeared on the scene, her friend had seemed shaken, come late to class, and scribbled in the margin of her notebook, "I'm going to commit suicide. J.M. has a new roommate." "Why did she do that?" I asked, puzzled. "She told us she was having an affair with you," my student answered. "Did the other students believe that?" "We did for a while," was her reply. So much for rule number one.

Then I began to understand the confrontation with that student which had occurred mid-year. We had been working together on several projects. I had thought her a friend, until she walked into my office. She couldn't work with me any more. I was exploiting her. I was a fascist. She was smiling. I looked at her, trying to decide between expressing my fury and the efficacy of a low key response. Could she be more specific, I asked, watching her tight grin. No. She had nothing else to say. Her attitude toward me the rest of that year was one of belligerent confrontation.

Since that day I have learned the phrase "hidden agenda," a catch-all expression for those expectations each of us carries around but seldom exposes to public scrutiny. For example, I have known what it is to be madly infatuated with someone.

But if she is involved elsewhere, hardly knows my name, can't stand to be around academics, my agenda—which insists that we will meet and make passionate love at the next feminist conference—remains hidden, must give way in the face of a reality that *is* out there somewhere. This student had lost track of reality. In lying about our relationship within her own peer community, she had taken an enormous risk, a risk I didn't understand at first. But it was a response to tensions she must have felt in my openly lesbian presence on campus.

In the beginning I had not understood my lesbianism would create such fear and tension. I had thought coming out was something I would do by myself, implicating only myself. I understand now that any woman who associates with me has to deal—in one way or another—with what that means to her. For a lesbian who dares not be exposed, associating with a "known" lesbian is extraordinarily risky. For those who are not even 'guilty,' association can feel risky. A married faculty woman with whom I have worked closely confessed this year that she was afraid to be seen sitting with me in faculty meetings. It was not a feeling she was proud of, but she *was* afraid. Students who are unsure of their own sexuality are threatened: I am a role model who says it's ok to be lesbian, implying a permission that can be liberating or terrifying. Students who are lesbian, but have not come out publicly, feel pushed to do so, by my example, creating fear and tensions. Originally, of course, I had expected only support from those who seemed logically to be my closest friends and community.

I don't think my example is a harmful one—far from it. Even when it causes fear and tension, I believe that stress can create an opportunity for growth that didn't exist so clearly before. Difference needs to be recognized and allowed to exist. But I have no prognosis of my own success or failure, which in this teaching career is measured by continued contracts and tenure. My work, much of which has a feminist or lesbian feminist perspective, will be judged by an institution which is by its very nature patriarchal and heterosexist. My open presence as a lesbian challenges many of the assumptions on which such an institution is based. And I will never know whether my work as a writer and teacher is being judged, or my life style. One of my colleagues has told me that my work with gay studies is looked on benignly: "I hope we're all open-minded here," he said. Another specifically said my perspective as a lesbian feminist was "too narrow for this department." The teaching half of my professional life depends upon the continued support of an institution.

As the "only lesbian professor" on campus, I feel isolated. Within my department and college, I have no peers, no one who shares my personal or political view of the world. Dealing with the alienation such a situation produces is consuming and exhausting, but the alienation of living a hidden life was far more debilitating to me. I don't really want to go back into the closet. It's too late. And too crowded. Living life in the open has been personally liberating and has felt enormously healthy. Not simple. Not without risk and challenge. But healthy.

ALIX DOBKIN

Lavender Jane Loves Women

In 1972, after more than ten years as a professional folk enter-
tainer who toured and sang all over the country, I decided to
sing women's music to women. Although at the time I knew
no one else who was singing it, women-identified music suited
me perfectly: I had recently come out as a lesbian, and my
feminist consciousness was expanding rapidly. I saw that many
of the tunes I had loved for many years had women-hating
lyrics. I needed new songs and a new audience to sing them for.

New York City seemed to be bursting with lesbian activity
in 1972. Several hundred women regularly showed up at
women's events, and my friend Liza and I were just beginning
to know some of them. Enthusiastic about any work which
touched on their lives, they welcomed my new material. When
I sang "A Woman's Love" for the first time at a lesbian feminist
liberation talent show, I was shaking so hard that I could hardly
breathe. Even so, the audience loved the song, as I knew they
would. I was thrilled to be writing in an original vein by docu-
menting my breathtaking growth as a lesbian. So much was
going on in women's lives as they hammered out new identities,
and hardly any of this new consciousness had found its way
into song.

In the spring of 1973, I noticed an attractive woman playing
flute at a women's skills festival which was held at the New
York City Women's Center. She joined me in a couple of folk
songs and played beautifully. I was impressed. We agreed to
meet to work out some material, and that was how Kay Gardner
and I began playing together.

We created simple arrangements of my songs, which we
played at small gatherings around town. Our audience was composed mainly of women who had come out or were thinking
about it. On one level or another, the message of feminist and
lesbian strength came through in most tunes. Some were less
controversial—old favorite folkies of mine—but I was becoming
more and more inspired to write music which reflected the
enormous changes I was going through. By playing this music,

Kay and I were filling, at least in part, a gap in the lives of women, and they loved us for it.

At that time, Jane Alpert was still in hiding from the F.B.I. She had released a public statement condemning the pretentious sexism of the male left and announcing her feminism. I thought she had done a great service to women by showing that men had drained our energies, and the name Lavender Jane reflected my appreciation.

Kay and I wanted a bottom for our music. We searched for cellists or bass players, but the women we found were scared away by our blatant lesbianism. The music is great, they said, but the politics too outrageous. We started making appeals for a bass player from the stage and finally, in August of 1973, after a gala coming out concert for *Lavender Jane*, several women approached us, propelling forward another woman. Her name was Pat and she played congas but wanted to learn bass. We were so overjoyed to find anyone who could consider playing with us that we nearly signed her up on the spot. We overwhelmed her doubts with our enthusiasm; we knew she could learn bass, and we convinced her of it.

Kay and I were constantly asked, "When are you going to make a record?" One night in September 1973 during a cruise on the Hudson River for five hundred lesbians, we were approached by a dozen of them who offered us enough money to make a lesbian record. It was a good place for *Lavender Jane* to be launched—a boatload of dancing and partying dykes listening to live music from the New Haven Women's Liberation Rock Band.

First we rehearsed with Pat. She got a tedious and frustrating cram course and within weeks she learned the eleven tunes she was to play on the album. Kay wrote string arrangements for three of the songs. I scouted around for a woman engineer, finally tracking down Marilyn Ries, who had been recording spoken material for years. When she turned out to be a lesbian we knew we were on the right track. We found musicians for the more elaborate arrangements and rehearsed with them. I wrote background material for the liner notes, and Kay and Pat wrote brief biographical notes. I doodled a drawing which became the cover and gathered information about how to make a record. Ellen Shumsky and Donna Glickman took photos. Liza agreed to look after my daughter, Adrian, and Kay's two daughters, Julie and Jenny. I filled out the copyright forms and researched royalty procedures. Nancy Johnson designed the insert which we used for the first thousand albums. We all worked enthusiastically as every element in the production fell into place.

Community support was very strong. Some women offered loans. From others we borrowed instruments, a bass for Pat and a twelve-string guitar for me. Many of our friends and most of our backers agreed to sing the choruses for two of the songs, and they loosely organized themselves into The Great Matriarchal Reunion. This group provided high spirits, lots of laughs, and better intonation than anyone had a right to expect.

Since the record was so much a part of our lives, Kay and I wanted our children to participate. "The Little House," which I had been singing for years, was a perfect vehicle for them and Jenny's friend Angie.

Marilyn worked in a small, minimally-equipped studio. We were all extremely nervous, and with good reason. None of us had ever made a record before, and our budget of $3,300 was laughably tiny by industry standards. But our women resources made up for our shortcomings. Most of the studio time, more than fifty hours, was spent by Kay, Marilyn, and me getting the best sound we could from the best takes we could make. The work was exciting, nerve-wracking, and intense. Sometimes it was boring. We finished the record late in November, 1973.

The three of us, together with Liza and other chorus members, formed Women's Music Network, Inc., to be a clearing house, booking agency, production company, publisher, and hub of women's music. Many hours were spent making grandiose plans for a nationwide, nonprofit, corporate empire of women's music. Since we had made a record from practically nothing, we felt that we could accomplish anything.

The first few Women's Music Network meetings were more like parties than meetings. We had one thousand records, one thousand blank jackets, one thousand inserts, and one thousand cover sheets. We folded, inserted, and pasted. Soon one thousand complete record albums were ready for sale.

My aims had been to get my music on record, to record "Jovanno" and "Eppie Morrie," which I had been saving for years, and to institutionalize lesbian culture. I wanted lesbians to finally have tangible musical proof of their existence. But how to get our pioneering record onto lesbians' turntables was a question I had never really considered, except for the decision to sell exclusively through women's and gay outlets. I was stumped.

The records had to be sold; Kay and I became business women fast. I was responsible for $3,500 in personal loans. We had to raise enough money through sales to finance printed jackets and more pressings. We examined the feminist press for names of outlets and found a surprising number of them. One of *Lavender Jane*'s most memorable concerts had been produced by a woman named Margaret Mercer, and we asked her to help us with the distribution. She agreed to work for a small fee, and somehow the three of us got the albums moving out, the money coming in, and the whole operation faintly resembling the beginnings of a business.

We struggled through our first year, learning as we went along. Universally praised in the women's and gay press, *Lavender Jane* was doing very well: the first pressing of one thousand records had sold out in less than three months. But Kay and I were having some conflicts about both music and money, and she decided to work on other projects (now there are good feelings between us again).

Meanwhile, Women's Music Network had become entangled in problems that came from a lack of energy and creative ideas and from our lack of a clear purpose. Realizing that Women's Music Network plans were unrealistic, Margaret and I established Project #1 to distribute *Lavender Jane*, and we officially separated from WMN in February of 1975. We found, though, that Project #1 could support only one person. Margaret and I had a perfectly amicable split, and I now operate the mail order business.

This method of distribution keeps me in touch with a large part of my audience through letters and orders. It also provides most of my marginal income. My records are still available only through women's and gay businesses—that way my music can help support them.

Lavender Jane, the first lesbian album produced entirely by women, gives me great delight and satisfaction. It is a wonderful record with a worldwide audience.

This article is excerpted from my book *Alix Dobkin's Adventures in Women's Music*, Tomato Publications, 1979.

BARBARA GRIER

The Garden Variety Lesbian

I came out at age twelve when I discovered that I was a lesbian. I did not know that word, of course, or the word homosexual. But I could tell my behavior patterns were different from those of my friends or the other young women around me, and I investigated in a quite sensible way for a fairly bright child: I went to the library and started looking.

I soon found the multi-syllabic word "homosexual," and while I didn't feel I fit any of the descriptions I was finding in the textbooks, there was enough similarity so that there was no question in my mind that I was being described. But instantly, even as I first made this discovery, I believed that the attitude in the books was entirely wrong.

I was a superior being, and I immediately felt that lesbianism explained why I had always felt superior. Something happened to reinforce my sense of this connection.

I was very close to my mother. I went home and told her that I was a lesbian. She treated it moderately lightly—that is, she said that since I was very young, that I was much too young for such an announcement. I should probably wait a few months at least before deciding that this was an absolute fact. But if it turned out that I was indeed a lesbian, then that was fine. The same things would be expected of me that I knew would always be expected of me. In other words, I was to be an honorable person in every way all of my life, and if I were honorable all of my life nothing but good would come to me. It was sort of a modified and less melodramatic version of Polonius' advice to Laertes. My mother supplied the name lesbian for me during this first conversation on the subject.

She simply started using the term "lesbian" and I automatically adopted it and have used it ever since. Mother and I talked about this several times in later years. At one point she wrote a nice long letter for the magazine *The Ladder* (before I was editor of it). It was very positive, very upbeat. She was in many ways an unusual person.

In a sense, that is all there was to my coming out. I came out.

I knew at age twelve that I was in love with my best friend. Her name was Barbara Shire. I also knew that it was unusual or different. I investigated it, I found a name or a handle for it. I went home and told my mother about it, and received, in effect, a parental blessing. And from that time on, I've lived as a lesbian, openly. I am positive that it is the reason that I have been extremely happy all of my life. I did have the required miserable teen years that we all live through. (When I say "all" I do not mean "all we lesbians" I mean "all we people.") Everyone seems to be unhappy to some extent during their teen years. I fell in love bunches of times then. I slept with perhaps ten to fifteen women between age twelve and seventeen. At age eighteen, I married for the first time. Another woman, of course.

Some humorous things happened to me through the years. I had a counselor in Colorado Springs High School, whose name I can't remember. She became very upset, not by the fact that I was a lesbian, but because I refused to keep it a secret. And I did upset her, to some extent. She would talk with me, then become so unnerved that she would cry and wring her hands and say, "Whatever will we do with you?" So I probably had some mildly traumatic experiences—that was, certainly.

And in the same city (Colorado Springs), one young woman, who was at least eight years older than I, started a conversation with me at a bus stop near my home. After we had seen each other perhaps a half a dozen times at the same bus stop, she learned that I was a lesbian and went home and told her mother. I would have been fifteen or sixteen years old then, fifteen probably. She would have been 23-24. She went home and told her mother that I was a lesbian and of course I have no way of knowing what kind of conversation they had. But I do know that about three days later, I was called to the counselor's office (the same counselor in Colorado Springs High School) and confronted by, of all people, two Police Officers from the Colorado Springs Police Department, who took me to the police station and for an hour or so badgered me with questions. Some of the ordinary, usual questions that we learn to accept and expect. Things like "What do you do with your girl friends?" in reference to genitals and so on, and even some things I hadn't heard of, and some suggestions that hadn't occurred to me, which I remember thinking about with curiosity. I realize now, of course, that this was all highly illegal. My parents were never notified. I was under age. I was threatened, coerced, and then dumped back in school with instructions never to speak to this particular woman again, and never to go near the place where she worked, a downtown theater. Now I had no interest in this young woman, which is rather remarkable, because I was interested in so many young women, but I was really annoyed by the ban on the Peak Theater, because I enjoyed that theater a lot. I resented having to give up one out of the five available theaters in downtown Colorado Springs.

My mother and I discussed this police event that took place in Colorado Springs when I was fifteen. But even though she was horrified, her horror had nothing to do with the gay aspects of it. What horrified her was that her daughter could even be taken to a police station. Remember in 1948, at least in my family, it was taken for granted that respectable people never had anything to do with the police—except if you lived to be old enough, you might be helped across the street by one sometime, or if you were very young you might have one standing guard at the crossing by your school. But certainly you were never arrested; you were never in any kind of intimate situation with a policeman.

Outside of that incident, I had some humorous and embarrassing things happen. The fact that I insisted on telling everyone I was a lesbian, everywhere I went, of course did create some social problems at times, but they were funny. After a certain point, shock actually has value, within the realms that the person is able to deal with shock. And, in those days, telling people you were a lesbian . . . I can't think of anything comparable today that would have the same effect. I did sort of create temporary catatonic states in people occasionally. But I enjoyed that. I mean that was like a weapon in the hands of a teenager. I was no different from any other teenager—that is to say, obnoxious, overbearing, arrogant, positive that I knew everything about everything. And my being a lesbian colored my teen years to some extent. One or two parents voiced objections to me; the rather sophisticated mother of one of the women I was interested in going to bed with when I was about sixteen objected to me to the extent that she walked her daughter back and forth to ice-skating practice at the arena at the Broadmoor in Colorado

Springs. Everything questionable certainly did happen to me in Colorado Springs. But nothing really eventful.

I went from Colorado Springs into Dodge City, Kansas, and then into Kansas City, Kansas, and graduated from high school in 1951. By that time, I had to help support my mother and my two younger sisters, so I went immediately from high school to work. Within a year of that time I had met and married Helen Bennett, and that was a very happy event. I went from a very promiscuous teenager to an absolutely monogamous and faithful, upright, uptight middle-class-type lover. Helen went to library school in Denver, and we came back to the Kansas City area because we both had parents there. For the next twenty years we very happily resided in the Middle West, in the Greater Kansas City area, either in Kansas City, Kansas, or across the river in Kansas City, Missouri. Now I am married to Donna McBride.

My public life, I guess, is pretty well known. I became an editor and a writer and I became an editor of *The Ladder*, a national lesbian magazine which began in San Francisco in the fifties. Before that I worked for *The Ladder* in various capacities. Through the years I went about still telling everybody in each clerical job I had that I was a lesbian and I never had any difficulty whatsoever with it.

I am absolutely convinced that if everyone would come out at once and stay out we could put an end to most of our problems. Everyone should come out and admit to themselves that they're lesbians and admit to everyone else they're lesbians. I do feel that there are areas of discretion: one does not force the idea on elderly people because in some cases they simply cannot comprehend what you're talking about. That's just a matter of bad taste, poor judgment. Other than that, I don't really think there is any excuse for not coming out. There might have been a few excuses when I was doing it in the early days. There were still, after all, some things that could happen to you, but now that there isn't much in the way of job security to worry about, I think we could end all of our oppressions immediately if we would just simply come out.

ELSA GIDLOW

France*

The sea voyage permitted me to draw more deeply into the still center of myself. In the belly of the pulsing ship as in a maternal body, with every physical need met, the spirit is free for undisturbed growing. For several of the seven days' journey, I rested in sleep or half-sleep from the recent months of worry and stress. I slowly found peace and inner quiet. In the body of the throbbing, rolling vessel, something was making me ready for the return to the continent of my origin. Did I belong to the Old World or the New? I felt that this was no casual pleasure trip. Would it be a search for my country (my place, myself?), my people (did they exist or must I help to bring them into being?), confirmation of the work I was destined to do (how to do it?).

After three days I woke to externals, the wells of energy refilled, eager for what lay ahead. I had been thrilled by the beauty of the great ship at first sight of her moving gently at anchor. Every water-riding vessel: slim canoe or squat tug, freighter or fishing boat, workaday tanker or luxurious liner: all excited me. Whatever their function or cargo, for me all bear a freight of dreams, rainbows of adventure, the dignity of daring powerful elements while gracefully accommodating to them. This ship, the ocean *Empress*, had gathered into herself my dream and daring. I felt possessive as I now explored her and surveyed my fellow passengers.

There were few in second class, mostly men and some elderly women. I had the luxury of a cabin to myself and was the only woman at my table. I noted two women, always together, whom I could not doubt were lesbian. I made no move to become acquainted. They were so angular and awkward in their absorption in deck games and one another. I saw no one who interested me and had only desultory, polite conversations. My quiet, con-

---

*An excerpt from *Elsa: I Come With My Songs*, by Elsa Gidlow; Celeste West, editor. Published in joint venture by Booklegger Press and Druid Heights Books (555 29th Street, San Francisco, CA 94131) in 1985.

tented love affair was with the ship and the sea.

Midway in the voyage, we folk in second class were invited to tour the upper reaches of first cabin and enjoy a concert by the Air Force Band. The luxury there was impressive, though I did not envy it. The concert was rousing, but I felt it was tactless to play "Britannia Rules the Waves" with storms brewing. It did not seem likely the waves would be intimidated, despite the Empire's presence on board in the persons of Sir Ramsey MacDonald and his daughter.

We arrived safely in Cherbourg. Marie met me in Paris. She helped me find an inexpensive room until I could choose a place for myself. I wondered what she, enjoying the opulence of her mother's place, thought of this room. It cost 375 francs with cement floor painted brown, and its walls papered with blue parrots sitting on beet-colored cabbages. The bed was spread with a rose quilt. There were curtains of crimson striped with yellow and the little writing table was covered with a cloth of rose pink with pale blue stripes. We did not speak of it. I was grateful to have a place to rest my luggage and sleep that night, but I knew I must find something else. I did: a quiet, simple room in a working class hotel far out on Rue de Vaugirard.

I could hardly wait to unpack before beginning to explore. The mazes of intricate, narrow streets, the old buildings whose stone faces and small windows were written over with history, drew me on whether or not I knew where I was going. It did not matter if I got lost; sooner or later I'd wind back to a familiar point and be ready to start in another direction. I felt immediately more at home than in Manhattan's arithmetic streets running in straight lines to office buildings and time clocks.

Marie, to celebrate my being there, took me for a feast of fine French food at an aristocratic restaurant. Thereafter, whenever she was on one of her long Paris visits with her mother, she repeated the gracious gesture, which I as graciously accepted. Looking at the prices on the menus, I saw that this Paris was closed to me on my 1,200 francs a month except as the recipient of a largesse which I could not repay in kind. But I felt so rich in my new freedom with no office waiting when I awoke, that I could envy no one.

I began to plan writing time for the early mornings. I resolved to work on a novel since there appeared to be so little demand

and payment for poetry. A publisher in New York had said to me, "Do a novel, get your name known that way, then we might consider the poetry." I did not really want to write novels. H. L. Mencken had asked to see some of my writing. When I showed him the poetry, he returned it, writing: "Do some articles for us." Poetry was the stepchild of literature in the marketplace. Why did it mean so much to me?

I was going to be more alone because Marie was returning to San Francisco. We had grown closer since seeing so much of one another, mainly at her mother's apartment talking far into midnight, drinking the *fine* she provided. Curiously, the growing affection I felt for her was without erotic excitement, what might be felt between sympathetic sisters.

She loaned me a book that was causing scandal and sensation, *The Well of Loneliness* by Radclyffe Hall. The author was involved in court suits over the lesbian novel. I was stirred by the story, though found it not very well done. In my journal I wrote: "It is a remarkable book, but I am sad because it might have been so much stronger. It was self-pitying, . . . pathos on the verge of bathos. The heroine, Stephen, takes herself with terrible solemnity, yet there are scenes in the book, many of them so real that I got cold shivers down my back." I added: "If the dramatic situations had been used for what they were worth, regardless of bourgeois morality, the book might have been great," rather than propaganda.

I knew nothing about the author. Imagining she might be a struggling writer like myself, I resolved to write to her, expressing appreciation for the courage it must have taken to so expose herself. With the letter, sent in care of her publisher, I enclosed several of my love poems to women. I had a hope that if she responded, I might meet women who would be my friends.

It was not until the first week in January that I heard from Radclyffe Hall. She wrote from London saying she expected to be in Paris in February, would like to see me, and talk about my work. It greatly excited me to personally meet another lesbian besides myself writing about our passions and tribulations. Alone on the literary island of heterosexuality, it was like sighting a friendly ship on the horizon.

Several months passed before we met, due to illnesses and her legal and other struggles with authorities over *The Well*.

Finally in March a letter came from a Miss Una Troubridge on behalf of Radclyffe Hall. Hall was convalescing from the influenza, but inquired if I would meet them for tea. I wondered about the "them." Was Miss T. her friend or secretary?

I met them both at the fine hotel where they were staying. A painful attack of shyness overtook me in the presence of their opulence, which I had not anticipated. I did my best to conceal it, but imagined I must be making a bad impression. Radclyffe Hall was older than I had expected; stocky of figure where I thought she would be tall, slim, athletic. The strong scent of violet perfume or toilet water preceded her as she welcomed me into the hotel sitting room and introduced me to Lady Troubridge.They led me upstairs to their rooms and ordered tea.

There I was surprised to see two birds in cages—Radclyffe Hall with caged birds! She wore a finely tailored brown suit with mannish shirt and tie. Her pale blond hair was cut as short as possible with inch-long sections combed down over each cheek. She had pearl earrings about the size of filberts, wore bracelets and half a dozen rings. So much feminine jewelry with an aspect otherwise masculine struck me as incongruous. My values then were more austere than now. I expected artists to be simpler, unconcerned with show.

Lady Troubridge also wore tailored clothes, but of a more feminine cut and even more jewelry than Radclyffe Hall. She was slim and handsome. Her iron-grey hair was cut page-boy fashion about a face still young. Her eyes, unlike Radclyffe Hall's which, although kind in their expression gave a message of deep suffering, were dark and smiling. Both had good legs and nice hands.

The birds twittered in their cages. The women, in their cages of class and privilege, questioned me politely about my writing. We sipped tea and nibbled the little cakes. I felt their graciousness conferred as from above. This inequality, unfounded on intrinsic worth, where I had hoped to find possibility of friendship, disappointed and saddened me. I was too proud to seek patronage, which I recognized was being offered as they asked to see more of my poetry, suggesting that they might be able to interest a London publisher in bringing out a book collection. I told them that I did not feel I had enough good work yet, that I was not writing poetry just then but prose. But I agreed to send them a copy of my book, *On a Grey Thread.*

We talked about Hall's work, the translations of *The Well.* She told me her own favorite of her work was an earlier novel, *The Unlit Lamp.* They spoke of perhaps visiting California, asked me about Los Angeles and prices there. They seemed very conscious of money. The more of it people have, the more they seem to worry about it.

I was now living in a new place where I could offer hospitality and, before leaving, invited them to tea. They were not sure how long they would be in Paris so no date was set. The tea engagement did not materialize although I saw them briefly on two later occasions. There were exchanges of letters and praises of my poetry (though no offer from their London publisher) continuing into my return to San Francisco. I still have the letters.

Since my stay in Paris was during the now legendary period of the Natalie Barney salon, the feverish fame of Renée Vivien and her poetry, and all the *épater le bourgeois* behaviors of the lesbian and other bohemian expatriates, I am frequently asked if I participated. I must say that I did not even know they existed until years later when I read about that colorful scene in the pages of *The Ladder.* It occurs to me that if I had been in Hall and Troubridge's position, encountering a young, and as they evidently thought, talented poet, obviously lonely, I would introduce her where she might find a compatible social environment. Was it snobbism that they did not even mention that such a group existed in Paris, and did they feel that my shoe-string existence would prove mutually embarrassing? Or, protectively, that my unsophistication might be corrupted? It probably is just as well. I was adventuresome enough to have got into emotionally difficult situations.

As time went on I did encounter a few lesbians, always paired. Kathryn Hulme, whom I had long been friends with in San Francisco, had come to live in Paris with her lover, Alice. Kathryn Hulme wrote *The Nun's Story,* among many other works. They had a comfortable flat and extended me the hospitality of their bath tub, a most welcome courtesy as a change from the daily cold sponges. At their flat I met the photographer Berenice Abbott and her friend Julia Perier. They introduced me to a handsome woman named Gwen LeGallienne. I never knew if she was related to Eva LeGallienne whom I had interviewed and written about while on *Pearson's*. She attracted me but I never really got to know her. When I saw her in the cafes or elsewhere she was with an interesting looking woman, the two evidently absorbed in one another.

At the studio of Berenice and Julia, I often encountered a young Frenchman, gentle and feminine, Jan Barbet-Manet. That acquaintance led to an extraordinary piece of good fortune. In voicing to him my delight in Paris, I had mentioned that in my otherwise satisfactory attic room I could not make meals. It was expensive eating in restaurants and I grew tired of the ones I could (barely) afford. A light came into his kindly young eyes as he said I must meet an Englishwoman he knew. Her name was Doris Penfold.

He brought us together one evening at Les Deux Maggots. She was from South Africa, well traveled, slightly older than myself, sprightly and cheerful, if somewhat timid and conventional. Doris had a friend from the United States, said to be a friend of T. E. Lawrence. This friend, now in Egypt, had a fully furnished flat in Montmartre which he occupied at most one or two of the summer months each year. He had urged Doris to live there, rent-free but for the minor expenses of gas, light, heat and tips to the concierge. She had never accepted, nervous about living alone. I expressed amazement that she should prefer living in a *pension*. She looked at me in equal astonishment that I would have leapt at such a boon.

"You mean you would—would you live there with me?"

"If I were asked." She not only asked, but joyfully urged.

We went together to look at it. I was enchanted: three spacious rooms, a kitchen, a bath (joy!), all comfortably furnished, including linens, cutlery, dishes, shelves of books, a gramophone, handsome Persian rugs—even a supply of Campbell's soups in the kitchen cupboard. (I left them there.)

I bade farewell to my little room at the top of the hotel at Rue de Vaugirard and to the friendly people there. In early February I moved into the sixth floor flat at 41 Rue Ramey. There I remained except for an early spring month of adventuring through France with Doris and a friend of hers who had the use of a car. No longer did I feel like a visitor. Doris Penfold would accept no rent, only my share of the expenses. She was away all day at the office where she worked, so I showed my gratitude by making the evening meal for us both.

Doing the marketing became a daily delight. I developed friendly relations with the women and men who had the street market stalls. It gave me pleasure after I returned home to hear from "Penny" that some of these would ask after me, "Where is Miss Gidlow?" (They never managed the hard G of my name.) I fell in love with the ordinary French people. All my encounters were warm, human, caring. If they learned that one was a student, a poet, there was an added friendliness. In the United States I had to hide the fact that I wrote poetry, especially in the world of business. This is a special kind of agony—not being able to share what is deepest in us, what we live by, our spiritually-sustaining source.

The French countryside, the human scale of the cities and towns, the architecture, the people of all classes fed me with such a sense of being at home in life. This came, I realize now, from a base of philosophically-informed common sense integrating the practical and the aesthetic, sexuality and soul, politics and spirituality. I did not feel an attitude of this or that. Rather it was a spontaneous acceptance of what worked *together.*

In all the little businesses, shops, enterprises, the *patronne* has as much, if not more, say than the *patron* in good natured give-and-take. Men did not feel it beneath them to push the baby carriage or do the marketing. Pairs of boys or young women walking together holding hands were friendly natural sights, as were mid-life or elderly women and men on the park benches embracing unselfconsciously. They were at home in their streets and cities where there was always somewhere to sit down. The half-humorous shrug at unpredictable events, or *c'est la vie,* expressed volumes of experience in reconciling differences between humans, humans and nature, humans and the fates. It all accorded with my feeling, unanalyzed then, that given right-heartedness, we humans should be as at ease in the world we were born of as was every other creature life had somehow spawned or evolved.

JANE RULE

Leave Taking

Moving around so much for the first twenty-five years of my life taught me to leave places lightly. Only when I was old enough to fall in love did places become linked with people and therefore invested with personal meaning for me. A particular street corner, the curve of a river might, even when it had been long deserted, resonate with lost joy. I can still weep at films of London streets or the sweep of the Sussex downs, particularly in B movies, but the experience of actually returning to that city or countryside has always been too rich in the present for there to be much room for nostalgia. "On this bridge," I can begin to think, but, if I'm not immediately distracted by the passing scene, I am as soon caught up in Helen's reactions, for she is both there with me and my companion of thirty years.

Still, I wondered when we planned a trip to New England last fall to Concord, Massachusetts, where we met and taught for two years, and to Lyme, New Hampshire, where Helen's mother had owned a farm, scene of family Christmases those years ago, and of a final summer, two years after she died, when we had to pack the place up and sell it. We hadn't been back for twenty years. Did I suggest my parents go with us partly as a way to keep the present sharply in focus? I did know, if there were to be nostalgia, Helen and I wouldn't share it as a common source. For Helen the eastern landscape is far richer in her past life and family than it is for me.

What we could all share was the purpose for going: the autumn color. Even the best photographs can't catch it, for though they show the whole landscape aflame in every color from the golds of birch, ash, elm, and aspen through oranges and pinks to the dark red of dogwood and red maple, they cannot provide the sharp clarity of air, scented with smoke and ripe apples, or show the drift and dance of leaves, or tempt the ear with the sound every child loves, the scrunch and scrabble of leaves underfoot, as loud as kicking at paper bags and yet sharp and fragile because one treads on the skeletons of leaves. After the humid heat of summer, the erupting lushness of that short season, the cool harvest air can also taste of the coming of snow. There is urgent, new energy to bring the crops in quickly, but it's crazed energy, too, in the flare of all that fragile dying. The pumpkins in the fields glow even in the dusk, and so do the apples on the already leafless trees.

I haven't remembered this from thirty years ago as the constant intoxication it is for me now. I can't imagine how anyone stays indoors, gets on with the job, why the whole village isn't out of doors at least, twirling and staggering into piles of leaves. Oh, there is an occasional berserk child, but the rest of Lyme, New Hampshire, goes on with its business, whether running the inn or the store, whether getting the church ready for a wedding or baking bread or milking the cows.

I do remember that industry, but they are mostly winter scenes in deep snow, the endless emergencies of furnaces going wrong in the chicken houses, of young stock free and headed to Hanover on the main road, none of which prevented people from getting to church, getting the Christmas dinner on or even sometimes reading by the fire in the book room, whose windows still had thick pine shutters to pull against raiding Indians.

And I remember summer, the heat, the relief of sudden storms, the dismantling of that beautiful old house, room by room, finding stashes of things undisturbed for the twenty-five years Helen's mother had lived there with her friend Florence, bottled fruits and vegetables in the cellar dating back to the war.

In autumn, I must have been at Concord, getting on with my teaching job. I do remember there the fields of pumpkins I saw from a train window on my way to Helen's house in Littleton, but I wouldn't have said my intoxication then had anything to do with the season.

How long has it been since I've been old enough to let the weather in, or in again as I must have when I was a child? And how long have I been old enough to return to such a place with no one left alive to call on? We do go to the cemetery to find Helen's mother's grave, all four of us, my parents a little shy of what that might mean to Helen, if not to me. I have never spoken extravagantly of my loves for parents other than my own, and I was raised by a woman who denies only one emotion: grief. I had not been there to bury Ruth, and Helen, concerned so much for the living as one is at such times, siblings, aging aunts, Florence, can't remember quite where the grave is. My mother is nervous to find it for her, stalks the rows of headstones without distraction because she does not recognize the number of names Helen and I do, the neighbors, the friends who belong to those long ago Christmases, even to the final auction when the farm was sold. My father detaches himself more easily, goes to take a picture of a young sugar maple, in full blaze, and it is under that tree we find Ruth's grave. Florence must have planted it there. Mother wants it to be a simple joy. Dad would like it to be his present, the finding and photographing. For Helen and me the complexities needn't be shared. Florence is not buried here. She must have been taken off by her sister, buried with relatives in Rochester, but her tree is here.

We all also go to the farm, down past the house we had renovated for Florence after Ruth died, past the chicken "prisons" as the family called them, past the barn next to the house, painted red now instead of white, a utility room added along the kitchen and dining room wall. We sold the place to a New York lawyer, the only one in those days with the money to buy it, $35,000 for an early settler's house, modernized and extended but itself at the core, for forty-some-odd acres and out-buildings. Four years ago a young family bought it for $235,000. They are in love with it, want to know every moment of its history back to its beginnings. The young wife welcomes us, asks us in. The living room seems smaller somehow, though there are the two-foot-wide pine boards, the old beams, and there are the words Ruth had carved over the fireplace, "Grow old along with me. The best is yet to be." The book room is as lived in as it was in the days we knew it. Helen will go back a couple of days later to talk about what she knows of the history of the house, a duty for her. I needn't go back, put my mind not to remembering but to worrying about that young family saddled with a killing mortgage. Obviously there is money in their families, but of the sort to provide expensive cars and holidays when they haven't operating money to keep the place warm in winter. But I suspect it has always been a struggle to live there, nearly a given in the harsh New Hampshire winters.

While Helen is away at the farm, I tend my mother who has come down with a heavy cold, and nearly absent-mindedly

I read the mood of the inn, where this morning we were given continental breakfast instead of the large country breakfast offered in the last few days. I assume it may simply be Sunday, which the owners take off, the woman not at the desk with her friendly banter, the man not cooking breakfast or tending bar.

The soups offered for dinner are too rich for an invalid's palate. The attentive substitute at the desk suggests we cross the green to the store and pick up a can of chicken soup which can be heated in the kitchen and a tray provided for Dad to take up to Mother before we have our own dinner. Helen, just back, volunteers to go, perhaps needing to stride out into quiet after her social afternoon.

We contemplate lobster for our own dinner. Helen hesitates and then is persuaded by Dad's enthusiasm. He is more talkative than usual at dinner, trying to make up for Mother's absence. Whenever we are all together, each of us has natural responsibilities, and Mother's is keeping us all amused.

At the end of the meal, just as I reach down for my handbag, Helen tips sideways from her chair. For a second, I think she has somehow simply lost her balance, but she is lying on her side, unconscious, a gash by her left eye made by her glasses, lying twisted and bloody beside her.

I am on my knees, trying to turn her oddly rigid body, trying to loosen the bow at her throat. A woman from another table in the dining room who is a nurse is down with us on the floor, taking Helen's pulse. She rouses but doesn't focus.

"Take deep breaths," the nurse instructs.

"What is it?" Helen asks, and I see her take in my face.

"You fainted," my father says, standing behind me.

She gags and swallows.

"I'm going to be sick."

"Take deep breaths."

I see her distress and embarrassment.

"Shall we help you to the bathroom?"

My father gets behind her and lifts her to her feet. The nurse and I on either side of her walk her toward the bathroom, but in the doorway of the hall she loses consciousness again, and I have to let her down gently against me to the floor, vomit flowing out of the side of her mouth into her hair, onto the floor.

Helen is conscious again, apologetic and bewildered. I clean the vomit from her hair with my hand, and Dad has found paper towels to clean up the floor. The woman on the desk has called the emergency crew. We've been able to move Helen to a couch by the time they arrive. They are giving her oxygen. They want to take her immediately to the hospital in Hanover, ten miles away. I am asked to get any medicine she's been taking. On the way back downstairs, I have only a moment to tell my mother what has happened, where we are going.

"I'll follow you," Dad says as I climb into the ambulance behind the stretcher.

As the ambulance swings out into the road, I feel the sour weight of my own undigested dinner and wonder if Helen will be sick again, but she seems all right, answering questions the attendant puts to her not only for information but to check her alertness. I hear in those questions concern for stroke, heart attack, diabetic attack. The attendant turns from Helen to radio instructions to the hospital. I can look out the back door of the ambulance and see my father at the wheel of our rented car, and I know his own nervous system is behaving just as mine does, in abeyance to will.

He has somehow parked the car and got to us before we go through the emergency entrance doors. When I am asked to provide information about insurance, he stays with Helen, holding her hand, smiling at her, and the attendants don't order him away, perhaps assuming he is her husband.

I have had enough experience in hospitals as "not next of kin" to be agreeable but assertive.

"I am next of kin," I say firmly.

"Relationship?"

"We've lived together for thirty years."

"The gentleman?"

"He's my father."

I have also had enough experience with emergency wards to be very impressed by this one, the efficiency and kindness of everyone dealing with us. We know the tests which are to be administered and why. We know how long they will take. We even know there is a possibility that Helen can be released when they're over.

Both my father and I need to clean up. The sour smell on my hands isn't offensive to me. It smells of Helen's life, and it is not the first time I've had its primitive reassurance.

We sit in the waiting room, neither of us talkative, but Dad again takes on Mother's role, as far as he can.

"Her color's good," he says. "At first I was frightened—a stroke or a heart attack, but I think she's going to be fine."

I haven't had time to be frightened, and I am nearly sure now that nothing serious is wrong, but I am glad of all the tests.

This is the hospital where, twenty-two years ago, Ruth died of kidney failure. Helen arrived in time to have her mother reach out, take her hand and say, "I'm taking this one with me," before she slipped into a final coma.

The tests are all negative. The doctor comes in to explain that it has been simply a temporary overloading of the nervous system, a tiring day perhaps? (I cannot know), a rich dinner, an attempt to stand up. It's unlikely to happen again. She needs only to rest for a day.

We're back at the inn just before ten o'clock. The kind woman at the desk says she planned to check on Mother herself if we weren't back soon.

"Thank you so much," I say.

"You're the one," she answers sympathetically. "I'm glad you're here to take care of them."

It is a remark Helen overhears on her way up the stairs.

"My poor darling, traveling with such a bunch of old crocks."

Dad lost a tooth just before we left, and we had to get him emergency dentistry.

I won't feel daunted. Hard jokes is all they are being, Dad's tooth, Mother's cold, Helen's fainting. I just don't want to be next.

It is Mother for whom the evening has been the most trying, lying there helpless to do anything but imagine the worst.

"You really must learn to drive again," she says to me, and I know she's buried Helen beside her mother and sent me home alone, incapable of caring for myself on our little island where there is no public transport.

I don't resent it. The interdependence and therefore self-sufficiency of any long devoted pair prompts other people to the bleakest image in an emergency. I've put my mother or my father under the sod more than once, a useless rehearsal of my own helplessness because my parents have never needed anything more than my easy love, and what would it be worth to either of them without the other? Something surely, but shamingly inadequate.

Mother and Helen rest on Monday. Dad goes out for solitary picture-taking. I go down to the parlor to take notes on the local trees, to read. Still the owners of the inn are not in evidence. We've had another continental breakfast, served by a young waitress in a sullen daze. The woman on duty for such a long day yesterday is here again today, looking strained and tired.

"Isn't it time you had a break?" I ask.

"Yes," she says. "I'm sorry about breakfast this morning. It isn't usually like this."

I wait.

"The owners' youngest son was killed in a car accident late Saturday night."

I had seen him on Saturday night at the desk talking to his mother, leaning over her with an unlit cigarette dangling from his mouth, a slight, tense boy of perhaps twenty.

"Since when do cigarettes cost $5.00?" she was asking, her tone light.

"I want a couple of beers. It's Saturday night."

I wondered what a twenty-year-old was doing bullying small sums of money from his mother, surly with her in front of guests.

"He seemed an unhappy kid," I say.

She nods. "Over the last few months . . ."

"It's a very hard age."

"Like my own boy. His father died when he was sixteen. Oh, he's all right now, quiet . . . sometimes too quiet. They were friends."

She needs to talk to someone not involved, where her own shocked feelings won't compete with more important griefs. She's had only a few hours' sleep in the last thirty-six. The boy was alone. The people in the other car were hurt, but they survived. He died soon after he got to the hospital. The two older sons are coming home. There will be a grave-side service tomorrow.

"The minister?"

"Oh, he's all right now that he's had some trouble of his own . . ."

When I knew Lyme, the woman minister shared the rectory

with a woman doctor who some time later killed herself, after they'd moved away.

A young couple come in to register. He pauses on the way up the stairs and asks, "Dress code?"

"Casual," the woman at the desk replies.

The phone rings. She answers, listens, says, "As well as can be expected. They got a little sleep last night."

Helen comes down the stairs in her coat. I put on my jacket and we walk across the green past the church to the store to find food for lunch we'll eat in our rooms. I tell her what has happened. On the counter there is a collection box for the dead boy. Helen puts money into it.

We will be gone, on our way to see old friends of my parents in Vermont, by the time he is buried tomorrow afternoon, too young to have learned to let the weather in, too young to have gone back to a place where everyone he's known lies in the graveyard, beneath the flaming trees.

I don't grieve for him. I grieve for his parents for whom he must now stay an unfinished spirit beyond their reach and help.

My mother would think it none of our business to take any part of that sorrow as our own. Enough to carry our own difficulties cheerfully into whatever is before us in Vermont, in Massachusetts, old friends, godchildren, nephews, lit by the light of the dying year.

But for me the present sucks up memory, the dead, love, grief, as gusts of wind suck up the leaves. I haven't any longer the heart for light leave taking. I think perhaps Helen never has.

BARBARA LIGHTNER

O! We Are Just Begun!

We'd been homesteading: a few animals, wild fruits and vegetables; chopping wood and hauling water; a garden. There was a clarity to life there and a strength in oneself in nature. In winter we tobogganed in with supplies. In summer we grew and gathered food for the winter. Everywhere Susan and I wove the colors of the seasons in our love.

But times changed. We didn't like the outside jobs we needed to support ourselves, we said; shit jobs. A farm was advertised for only $250 an acre. And the farmer was 78, too old to carry the feed around anymore. If we'd carry the feed, he'd teach us to milk and, after we learned to milk, give us some of the check.

II

We name our living into the working of our days. There was an ungainly cow who produced large quantities of thick, rich milk. Next to her was a tiny small-boned cow, very dark around the face. They were Gertrude and Alice B.

Another cow was a nightmare mixture of black and white: she was Djuna in the Barnes. Miss Brown resembled in her fastidiousness one of a pair of two loving headmistresses I'd had in grade school. And though neither Susan nor I played pool, we honored those who did with Eight-in-the-Side-Pocket—she never went where she was s'posed to go.

Our darlin' Clem let anybody ride her and was the peoples' cow. Hadley, even though we'd never known a Hadley at the schools a Hadley must have gone to, was the very best our nation's boarding schools have to offer. Sudabaker was the stringy, strongest, toughest cow, not a regular cow at all; as Sudabaker, the small black child I knew in my youth in the south, was stringy and tough and not regular and somehow always the meaning of my guilt. Maude with calf was me on welfare. She had to be sent away because the radical surgery needed to save her life was not "economically feasible."

The goose paraded up and down, as if telling by the bob of her head who belonged to this money-making operation. She was Perle Mesta. Wilhemena the pig farrowed her first time with twelve who lived—a laudable record even for an experienced sow. She was for reasons perhaps clear only to me the Wilhemena of sixth grade, in a school I hated in the south, who proved her engagement ring a diamond by scratching it across somebody's compact mirror. Everybody looked askance at Wilhemena for doing just a little bit too early, and vulgarly, what everybody would do later, delicately. I had liked Wilhemena a lot.

While naming our working, we learned to shovel shit for fifty cows, the sow and a bull. Susan and I will both attest to it, bull shit is the heaviest of all.

III

It came time to make the farm possible. Our first stop was the Ag Extension agent. "We've found a dairy farm," we said; "The retiring farmer will stay on and help us. If we have 70 tillable acres, how many cows . . ."

"Why don't you go to beef? Have you ever thought of pigs? I just hate to think of women"—and he extends the phrase as if holding something unpleasant in tweezers—"shovelling all that, ahem."

"But pigs defecate, too," we said with the tweezers. "We're interested in cows."

It was a time when neither beef nor pigs would make a farmer's living. Dairying was the only alternative.

IV

Our second stop was the Farm Home Administration for a loan. We are the ideal candidates. "There is no way," we are told, "you can get a loan."

And there is no way we can fight him. Don't even know how to go about proving he should be fought. A friend graduates from law school soon. But how could we support her while she makes a case for us?

V

"Women are learning to support and help women," Donna once said. She lends us the money to buy seven cows.

Judy looks at the aerial photographs of the farm and thinks

she might have enough money for five. She comes to visit and thinks she might have enough for "a good even dozen." Then Alice sends the downpayment on a tractor and Donna adds the money for seven more cows. Dede offers to invest in some of the wooded acres to help with a downpayment on the land.

The women from the Christmas tree farm come down to teach us to butcher. The vet's receptionist answers questions the vet cannot. And the city-bred psychiatrist outdoes the seasoned farmer when she suggests a furniture clamp to hold the milking claw together.

Sometimes we hesitate; there is so much to be known in this beginning. But we are milking now and learning to manage, supported in this male-directed world by a community of women.

VI

About one farming arrangement the book says, "The landlord has little or no management responsibility . . . This type of lease is most desirable for women." No management responsibility.

Management, the splitting off of brain from brawn. A male tells us that we can probably do the physical labor but "women can't handle the management."

Management plans what crops go in which fields, which cows are bought and which ones sold, consults the lawyer in matters of estate planning. Then, when all is done, and with a judicious shake of the head, the manager does what the neighbors do. Women can't handle the management.

But the men went off to war, the women managed. The men sought love and glory in King Arthur's court, the women managed. Brother fought brother in the Civil War and women managed.

"It's wonderful, of course! But however will you manage, you two out there all alone?"

"You don't know anything about management," Walter said when we told him. "You can't seed the bottom to alfalfa. It'll get too coarse and stemmy."

"Even if we cut it early?"

"Even if you cut it early."

We seed the bottom to alfalfa. The first crop we cut early so it won't be coarse and stemmy. The second crop, because it's in a bottom, thrives through the drought and we have hay for the winter. We've handled the management.

And O! We are just begun!

VII

We continue working and learning. We learn to know each cow well enough to tell by the slightest variation that she is sick. We learn it is not worth worrying about keeping the bull. We learn that when we visit friends it is best to stay awake until 4:00 in the morning, then make the two-hour drive back for morning milking at 6:00.

We learn how to fix the manure spreader in below freezing weather in less than an hour and a half; and how to string fence, and how to pull calves, and what it's like to keep vigil all night when the sow farrows.

Lightning strikes the silo one morning and runs down it and jumps to Susan and throws her on the floor. We learn how to accept hurt.

And we learn yelling and screaming at each other because we are scared and don't always know what to do and there is no one to tell us or make it all right, and we don't have the confidence to know it will be all right because neither of us—not even anyone we know—has ever been a farmer.

VIII

We settle into a pattern of our days. Weekends are for auctions. We go to buy canning jars and cows. Nights are for reading and planning. From looking at the mixed bag of cows we have in the barn, Susan and I decide we will buy Jerseys. Jerseys are small cows with thick, rich milk. They are tawny brown, lovely on the green hills of pasture. Some 90 percent of farmers have Holsteins because they "fit the market" better—they give lots of milk, never mind its inferior quality; and their calves are big (you sell all bull calves immediately) so bring more on the market. But the big, flashy, black and white Holstein with all its poor quality milk strikes us as somehow too typical of what is crass in America. So we spend our time planning around Jerseys and hope we can make it.

We also, at least in the beginning, save the one night a week the town library is open. Out of the much it doesn't have, this one has a full collection of Wisconsin's very own famous woman, Zona Gale. We special order *Flying* and get it—along with critical side glances. But then the library changes hands, someone plants petunias in the shape of the flag, the atmosphere changes, and we no longer get our special orders. We no longer save that one night a week.

IX

We also discover there is time to think about things, plenty of it—during milking and feeding and fixing and ploughing and seeding and harvesting and driving the long drive to the feed mill. Susan and I do not work together often. The sheer number of tasks demands an end to idyllic dreams and sets the need for us to split ourselves among the jobs to be done. So there is plenty of time for thinking, solitary thinking.

Some days the thinking is awful. There's never enough money to cover. And there's always a sick cow. Calves from the best cows die. And the bank wants its money.

Or hail is predicted and you know two minutes of hail will be the end of the corn. Or a wind will flatten the oats. Or no rain comes. Or an ice storm puts out the electricity and there is no way to hand milk 50 cows who then suffer terrible, painful inflammations. Or a cow goes down in the barn and can't get up, and you have to stand there and watch them shoot her and drag her heedlessly out.

Other days, though, out of this solitary thinking, comes a new knowledge, one of ourselves as woman. From the goddess-worshipping societies we know Iris, Ceres, Hathor. Hathor, funny goddess, the cow goddess whose legs are the four pillars of the earth. And the pig comes to us as sacred.

Not that we participate in farming as sacrament. But we learn of a tradition behind us, learn woman. And we learn that we are not deprived of the cunning and practicality associated with the farmer. A woman has invented the cotton gin. A woman has invented the first milking machine. And a woman we know has taught us the uses of the furniture clamp.

Susan and I stagger the chores so there is time to write; and one morning I write:

FIAT

Who ordains this world
in her infinite wisdom
is woman
does not do a bad job
for having come again lately
and without benefit of
kingdom and power and glory
or myth or miracle to speed tasks along
in a week
with a day off for rest;
who is innumerable selves
out of this world's precursed paradise
and women walking lovely in green wood
to whom we give dominion
glory love
ourselves
in new beginning
in second coming

X

We farm, however, in a real world. And there are antirhythms
to our life.

"If you're going to farm and be men," the friendly shoe sales-
man said, "then you have to buy men's shoes."

We answer: when there are all those boots you don't want to
walk in and all those footsteps you don't want to follow?

Farming, once lovely, now also hinged round by patriarchal
pride. "I married my woman to cook and keep house. That's
what she's supposed to do and that's what she done," Winchell
said, daring us to answer that one.

XI

And there is Thelma who is also part of this real world. "My
mother always said a good woman's got to like water and here
I am hating to wash dishes, hating water," Thelma said. "Maybe
I oughta been a boy," she added, not altogether laughing,
nevertheless laughing; caught by farmers like Winchell and by
a fiction of inferiority.

"Anyway, what do I know," she continued, using the only

logic available to her in her isolation, "being as I'm just a woman, hating water that way. And my husband such a good man. And me such a bad woman."

Thelma: never been out of the state. Never stepped out of her role. Living way back in, down such a long gravel road, where so few come to tell her of her own fine strength.

XII

"No change never hurts too much," Cora agreed and told her husband, as she had not done before, to get his own ice cream.

"But if you know anything at all," he said in what only seemed a nonsequitur, mad now at having to get his own ice cream —"if you know anything at all—you have to face the fact that the bull makes the herd."

It is an old farming maxim.

We know only these murmuring, mammary beasts, analogue to archetypal matriarchy, the bull brought in for service; excellence assumed in matrilineal descent, bull's proof taken from dam and daughters.

It is our beginning and, even in this real world of farming, our new kind of knowing.

ROSEMARY CURB

"Remember the Future"

This morning I sat at the opening faculty meeting of the southern state college where I teach English, crossing and uncrossing my panti-hosed legs and folding and unfolding my arms over the large pewter labyris ⟨⟩ dangling down the center of the same prim white T-shirt in which I stormed the capitol for equal rights a month and a half ago. This morning a Chamber of Commerce representative assured the rows of polished bald heads that the business community is concerned not only about business expansion but about preserving our American way of life, Christian morality and the family. Knowing the hatred and bigotry behind such glittering exhibitions of patriotism, I shudder.

Less than a week ago I was glowing with vitality at the Michigan Womyn's Music Festival. To cross the miles and centuries from that woodsy womanspace, with beautiful Amazons leaping naked through the trees and dancing barefoot in the grass, to this bastion of male power paralyzes my womansoul. This morning I wore a long billowy India print skirt with intricate designs in lavender, mustard, indigo and ivory. Perhaps I should have encased my womansoftness in an exoskeleton of armor. I feel in my own flesh the loss of the ancient matriarchy. My labyris, with "Remember the Future" etched on its back, consoles me here in patriarchal exile. I know in my nerves and tendons that I am not part of this oppressive system even though I endure imprisonment here.

Although my spirit aches with remembrance of the year ahead, I must gather strength from woman-shared moments this summer of leisure and celebration—the first non-academic summer I can remember in twenty years.

My golden friend Anna and I arrived at the Michigan festival late Thursday. In the midst of our first concert, I have a revolutionary idea: every woman at the festival ought to address each woman in her life as "sister." I am not sure I can do it, but it would imply universal sisterhood. I remember in the convent the warmth I felt when I was first called "Sister."

This morning I arrived after the Chamber of Commerce speech had begun and missed my chance for a chair. A carefully-groomed woman smiled at me from her back row seat and motioned to me to share it. I declined—cautious about getting too close, I suppose—but yes, it would have been easy enough to address her as "Sister," and I don't think she would have fainted or been eaten up with suspicion. A moment later a short bustling woman who always calls me "Dear" squeezed me on the arm. Could I call her "Sister"? Two men rose from the row ahead of us and more than offered, they forced us to take their seats. The fifty-year-old history professor holding my arm murmured "Wasn't that nice?" in my ear as we slid into the seats. A man behind us chortled for our benefit: "damn women!"—an attempt at humor, I suppose, based on the commonly-held male chauvinist notion that after all their impudent talk about women's liberation and equal rights women really in their little pink powder puff hearts still want to be treated like dolls and have doors opened for them, seats relinquished, and above all, meals and drinks paid for by men, whose apelike muscularity will emphasize our sugary feminine fragility. "Damn men!" I thought. I tried to tune out the Chamber of Commerce pep talk.

Ah! I am there again at the festival . . . What a rush of pleasure to see clusters of women everywhere. I feel washing clean in the swirl of womanenergy. Supper is roasted corn, crisp salad vegetables with yoghurt dressing, dark brown bread with peanut butter or tahini, and watermelon. There is a woman wearing nothing but a tie whose triangular tip is brushing her pubic hair. How chic! Several women are wearing only belts with knives in rugged leather cases. Since I need a collection of pockets, I may not make it as a naked Amazon, but I love being a spectator here.

Friday mid-morning rain patters loudly on our camper roof while we snuggle cozily inside with books and tin mugs of coffee still hot from our airpot filled yesterday in Holland. When the sky clears, I can't find lesbian writers reading from their works, so Anna and I settle for a systematic survey of the merchants' wares. It certainly doesn't feel like the Mall shopping center near my college. Although these women accept Master Charge and checks as well as the folding green (stamped perhaps "lesbian money"), the whole commercial atmosphere is charged with a sense of dedication to the coming Matriarchy where ripping off will be obsolete. Sellers casually leave whole boxes of T-shirts and other goods unattended, with little fear of theft by their sisters. I buy my giant pewter labyris, and a smaller ceramic model, a feminist Wicca shirt, and a book by Z Budapest.

I run into a friend who tells me about problems with her lover, a celebrity—how she feels frightened, resentful, and diminished by the overpowering older woman. Why do women who love each other passionately, as Anna and I do, hurt each other so frequently and with such apparently defensive malice? When Anna seems to freeze me out, I feel crazy and violent, and I want to hurt and destroy everything—especially myself. Not only do we remember the future, but we anticipate the past in our recurring quarrels. Perhaps we don't love ourselves enough or believe that we are truly lovable.

Feeling the need for some sort of spiritual renewal, I join a workshop on Cycles and Rituals, but I can't let myself go. The young women, mostly naked and enjoying their unfettered beautiful bodies, are as exuberant and uninhibited as I once was, and those greyhaired and lined—older than I—seem very strong and wise. I am curious about a workshop titled "Anger" because I have so much of it. But, even more, I need space away from the throng, and so I return to the camper to be alone.

Rain cuts short the Friday evening concert. Thunder, lightning and threats of tornadoes bombard us all night. Anna and I hug each other to sleep feeling in our closeness a deep joy that we haven't quarreled at all on this trip, as we had feared we would.

By Saturday morning the torrents have stopped, and I've lost track of time. It seems we've nibbled some lotus flowers of forgetfulness. Where is home? It must be here. Please, goddess, let us stay in this womanspace forever.

My tin plate filled with a generous portion of granola and creamy yoghurt, I go off to the Lesbian Parenting Workshop. Dee, the facilitator, is compiling data on custody battles of lesbian mothers and wants to hear horror stories from us about the evil machinations of the "justice" system. But the eight of us who attend the workshop are fairly satisfied with our living situations. At least I've no custody problems.

One woman seems to cling to the respectability which heterosexuality brings. I am ashamed to admit how long I spent in that stage, before I could let go of men and of all the rewards I thought I got from being part of the patriarchy. Two women lovers at the workshop say that they have four children. I like it that they don't say whose children are whose biologically.

I am late arriving at the Lesbian Writers Workshops. The young women there are dreamy intense types with notebooks and folders of poems. I do not hear the Adrienne Rich of the coming generation, but maybe I'm not listening hard enough. I read from my journal on the Champaign festival, and they all laugh just as my friends did. Glowing, I dash back to the merchants' tent to tend the Matriarchy booth. I find how pleasant it is to preach matriarchy to the already converted.

One of the constant delights of the festival is discovering clusters of women musicians, who perhaps just met each other five minutes before, jamming together on their various instruments. Women with flutes send forth a haunting womantone from under a huge maternal maple. Drummers advise each other on technique. Musicians of some renown who are not on the evening program (such as Casse Culver) attract a crowd in the rehearsal tent near our camper. Lying in our camper bed Saturday afternoon, we watch lithe female bodies leap across the sky while Casse, in that peculiar yodel that is her trademark, sings "We were lovers to the music of the country radio in our 4 by 8 foot run-down camper van."

Sunday morning I make coffee on our hibachi. As planned, Dee comes to interview me at ten for her study on lesbian mothers. We talk for over two hours because I answer every question in voluminous detail. In one question, for example, she asks me to trace the history of my sex life. She wants to assess my personal attitudes and habits but even more my philosophy of childrearing. I conclude our interview by declaring that lesbians are potentially better mothers than nonlesbians because they present their children—especially their daughters—with a strong independent female role model. Dee leaves me with a 480-question California Personality Inventory to complete. It is amusing and somehow gratifying to see all the academic paraphernalia out in the woods.

When I finish my questionnaire, I scramble off to Liz's workshop on matriarchy. The discussion has digressed to food, and women are eagerly confessing their addictions to tobacco and caffeine. The Festival has provided only healthy food—no meat, and not a french fry, a Dorito, or a Twinkie on the grounds, unless they're smuggled in.

We never get to one issue: how we can be true to the matriarchy while working within the patriarchal system. The question troubles me, since I am paid by the state, although I do not reinforce patriarchal attitudes as I teach literature. Rather, I try to open students' minds to the system of oppression revealed in literature. After all, literature mirrors our lives, present and past. Although I resent having been indoctrinated by patriarchal beliefs, I am joyfully relearning everything from a matriarchal viewpoint.

Oh yes, with the naive docility encouraged by our educational system, public and parochial, I had gulped down as "divine revelation" not only the biblical story about the fall of man, but even the so-called "natural" order of male dominance in the pantheon of Greek deities. Daddy Zeus wields thunderbolts and "playfully" rapes those mortal maidens foolish enough to frolic in the joy of their blossoming bodies under his all-seeing lustful gaze. Which current womenenergy was it that recharged all that information in the new light of matriarchy? Was it *The First Sex* by Elizabeth Gould Davis? *Beyond God the Father* by Mary Daly? *The Dialectic of Sex* by Shulamith Firestone? *Mothers and Amazons* by Helen Diner? *When God was a Woman* by Merlin Stone? All of the above. Yes. Now teach Genesis for what it is: a defensively paranoid misogynist tract against Goddess worship, Matriarchy, and the whole female sex. Of course, misogyny at the roots of Greek and Hebrew culture is ultimately responsible for the sexism in British and American literature, from Milton to Mailer and all those boys. I name the education that I gobbled up for so many years BULLSHIT, and I'm still vomiting up the patriarchal decree which says that women who live outside the law of male domination must be punished/ridiculed/condemned.

Sunday evening is the end of the festival. Sleeping bag bunched under my arm, I assure Anna that I'll find an ideal spot for the grand finale, even though I can see that the entire valley is occupied. I stake out a spot on a grassy slope with knee and elbow room and even a young sapling. But when we settle in for the concert of Meg Christian and Teresa Trull, I realize that I've positioned us for an excellent view of the left speakers and the mixing board but not a glimpse of the performers. Oh well, we've seen Meg and Teresa before.

Sweet Honey in the Rock is as magnificent a musical treat as we had hoped. One of the women in the group presents the idea that becomes the key of my reminiscences: where we will be on Tuesday morning will be much different from where we are now. How painfully true! If I can remember the future, can I anticipate the past? How will the present feel in the future when it is past? In my head I can hear the dissonant sadness of the opening line of "The Return of the Great Mother"—"We have lost our dreams." Oh no, make them happen.

The next morning the hollowness of the ending hits full force. We hear the rumble of wheels on the dirt road and voices shouting, "Goodbye, all you beautiful women." I find several reasons to walk back and forth across the main meadow to wash our dishes and fill our water jug. I can't believe the festival is over. Walking out I feel like I used to at the end of a Girl Scout camp session—refreshed and exhausted as if I'd had a brisk swim.

Now in exile from the past and future dream of women sharing work and joy and love, I must hold myself together to nurture those who need me in my professional public role. My students will come to me saturated with banal tastes and prejudice. I must lead them lovingly, gently, but fiercely toward the dawn of matriarchy in our time. May the goddess glow through me and may all the strong women of the past invigorate me.

NOTE: The horrors Rosemary Curb anticipates in this piece were realized in the 1978-79 school year when she xeroxed a similar work at her college in Missouri and was reprimanded by the administration for using school equipment to reproduce a "lewd" story. Eventually she was fired. She now teaches in Florida, in happier surroundings.

JUDITH NIEMI

Hudson Bay Journal

In July 1978 six Minnesota dykes canoed to Hudson Bay, paddling and portaging 380 miles along an old route where we were the only travellers. We weren't all experienced canoeists, or even in great physical shape when we started—just a group of friends who wanted to experience challenge and adventure together. We didn't exactly plan it, but were excited to find that we were the first all-woman group to arrive at York Factory. About time.

We now have very different perceptions of the trip, and this is my version of it; still, when I read July thoughts I don't know whose they are. Our common property. These excerpts are from a journal I kept then and in the following weeks to try to remember the trip, remember how I was, and think about what being a dyke had to do with it.

DAY 1   CROSS LAKE. First campsite, a pink and violet granite shelf, thrushes singing across the channel, four of us writing in our journals. This afternoon when we were finally on the lake I felt suddenly calm, at home. "Prayerful" too, I thought, and that's a word I haven't used for twenty years—a recognition that what we're doing seems big, an act of faith. As we paddled off Connie said, "Think how many women in Minneapolis are thinking about us today."

UNDATED ENTRY. For me this trip is fulfilling a fantasy. For years I've wanted to make a long canoe trip and didn't do anything about it. Then on a ski weekend a group of women started talking about our dreams, taking ourselves seriously, I guess. I said out loud that I wanted to canoe to Hudson Bay, and Jean instantly said, "I'll go with you, Judith." We're both too old not to start doing what we want.

I'm pleased that in recruiting other women we decided not to look for expertise and muscle but for women we wanted to share the experience with. At our first we're-really-going-to-do-this meeting last December Jean said, "Well, I want to go with feminists—not someone who'll sit around the campfire and say 'Gee whiz, isn't it great to be just us women!' " "What would

204 / The Lesbian Path

an opening campfire line be?" "Oh, maybe 'This is what the matriarchy was like, I just know it.'"

It wasn't hard to find women volunteering to come along. We have discussed our greatest fears, and what our personal low threshholds are (bugs, tired wet feet, rain) and each packed accordingly. We had a group chart done by Moonrabbit, who tells us there are so many fixed signs among us we have to remember to have fun, there's no doubt we'll hang in there. And suggests who not paddle with who in the rapids. We plan to live "tribally," and to find out by doing it what we mean by that.

DAY 5   CROSS LAKE. MUCK. After a late afternoon dinner we come to the shallow bay where Real Berard's map, our only source of information, tells us we may have to wade the canoes for several miles. Connie splashes onto a big rock to scout, shrieks and collapses when she sees only waving green reeds in all directions. We find a narrow channel marked with a birch pole and start a long evening of wading knee deep in fine muck. Dead jackfish float belly up, and sometimes ooze out under our bare toes. This is not Nature we are fighting with, but Manitoba hydro—the new dam at Jenpeg has lowered the lake level about ten feet, ruining the fishing, angering the local Crees, and certainly complicating this route. The patriarchy as usual messing things up because it thinks it needs more of what it thinks is power.

At sunset we make our first emergency camp on the mud flats, unloading only sleeping bags, one tent, the Svea stove. The Lesbian Grooming Authority decrees that we let the mud dry on our legs and scrape it off with Swiss army knives before entering the tent.

Scene in a bog: incredible scarlet sunset over the boreal forest. Mosquitos rise in clouds from the drained lake bed. Three canoes lie heavily, stranded far out in the muck. Through the swamp grasses two tiny heads appear, Kristin and Connie, squatting sociably. "Considering the options, this isn't a bad campsite." "No, actually it's quite nice." Jean and I overhearing this get pretty hysterical.

In the morning Jean is up early hiking on the mud flats, and comes back to report several more miles of this. We agree to stick with our present canoe partners however long it takes us to get through this. Lorry and I become Muck Sisters. Lorry and I were also together a couple days ago to see something floating in the shallows that looked like a bloated moose haunch until we got closer. "Look at the feet—it has toes!" Well, it might have been a bear. Or a human. We didn't care to check.

UNDATED ENTRY. Until the muck, I couldn't totally believe in the trip. Too many closeted years of thinking no one shared my visions. That hold-out untrusting part of me secretly believed someone would say, "This is too hard. Let's go back and just take the train to Churchill." But my friends were trucking on, kvetching, smiling, inventing madrigals—"Mucky wa-aa-a-aters." Faith cautiously settled down on me. Besides, no one would ever consider going *back* through that muck.

DAY 7 ELIZABETH CADY STANTON LAKE or SUSAN-NAH MOODY LAKE—THE UNNAMED LAKE AFTER THE PORTAGE. We have been thinking the casual directions our map gives for finding the portage into the next watershed are pretty funny, challengingly vague: "in a jackpine cluster by a large rock." Now that we're at the end of this dried-up bay we spend all late afternoon and evening searching jackpine clusters and rocks—nothing. In the morning we collect our wits, pool our information, and organize three parties to search the other branch of the beaver stream. Four of us have the fun of finding the trail.

It was scary and frustrating for a while, but I loved the search. After the muck to be in sweet-smelling pines, hiking alone across the hummocks in the low light, I felt free in a beautiful land, unlimited space all around me. I was also so exhausted that when I saw my very own Muck Sister across the beaver stream that evening I couldn't recall her name or face.

The portage is two miles through a peat bog (where it gets especially nasty, we name it the Richard M. Nixon Memorial Bog). The trail is worn deep in the sphagnum moss, a path used by Crees since York Factory was established in 1693, probably before that.

It's a day's work to get everything across. On my second trip with a canoe I find my second wind and feel elated, euphoric. We're all very tired when we're done, I suppose that at 27 to 41 we don't have the resilience of kids. But we're all better than we used to be. Tougher. Beautiful leathery tanned faces, scuffed up legs. We're going to make it.

UNDATED. The carrying is slowed up because Connie and Aurora can't carry heavy loads. In March Connie broke her ankle and it's not strong yet. Two weeks before we left Aurora put out her back again, could hardly walk. Crises. Each of them decided to risk the trip and the rest of decided we're willing to carry extra.

It fits the way we want to travel. We chose not the Hayes River, easier, more travelled, where the European explorers pushed into the interior of the continent in York boats, but an older Indian route on the Bigstone and Fox Rivers, suitable only for small canoes. The British explorers did this heroic military stuff, travelling at top speed to get somewhere else. The Crees lived here, and when they went to York Factory to trade, the whole group went, women, men, children, aged people.

Our "crips" have done almost all the food packing and are head cooks. Sugar-free, vegetarian food, no additives. One day Connie gets hilarious inventorying the contents of Aurora's handy bag of Necessities: agar agar, chia seed, black bean powder, hijiki, daikon, seaweed. . . .

DAY 10 BEAR LAKE. ALICE B. TOKLAS CAMP. Most difficult campsite yet. A day of riding huge rollers in a tailwind ends as we paddle around bouldery islands looking for any little clearing to camp in. We land in waves and spray at a tiny opening in the tangle of spruce and Labrador Tea. We've been up since early for once, and it's now last light, maybe ten or eleven, but after hacking out space for one tent, we fix *two* gourmet dinners, Asian rice and noodles-with-something, put wild roses in a Sierra cup for a centerpiece, eat by candlelight. Dinner music—Lorry plays Morley songs on the flute and I try to sing along, "Flora, beauteous and fair alas hath slain mee."

We're getting fond of this one-tent method of camping—it's no longer "emergency," just the Alice B. Toklas Alternative. Four of us share two zipped-together sleeping bags. What would male fantasies be of what six lesbians do in a tent? What we are actually doing right now is talking about the ospreys and bald eagles we saw.

UNDATED. Canoeing conversation: Connie said the other day she hadn't once had to think about being a lesbian or being political. For once we have no opposition, an opportunity to

take ourselves for granted and live without self-consciousness.
For me being here at all is only because I'm a lesbian. Something
about being myself, trust, and knowing risk-taking is not for
thrills, but a necessary survival skill.

We think of the other world only rarely. We wonder if men
ever compliment each other on a big fish and then ask, "What
color stringer do you want?" Dragonflies mating in the air remind us that Anita Bryant claimed in that *Playboy* interview
that sex with Bob is like "Christ meeting the church in the air."
Truly bizarre. Apologies, dragonflies. Jean has invented an an-
thropologist who observes us, writing up his doltish field notes:
"In the evening they can be observed clustering together on
rocks, grooming each other and hugging." But that's about all
the attention the straight world gets from us. We don't even
miss our friends.

DAY 12 BIGSTONE LAKE. WINDBOUND. A gale from the
North, cold wind, huge waves—we have no choice but to rest.
130 miles behind us, and over 250 miles to go before we meet
a plane only 14 days from now. It takes four of us a while to
get a fire going without using any white gas. We feast on millet
and ground barley and decide to enjoy the layover, sleeping,
reading, drying clothes, sorting out gear. We take a canoe out
in the storm to pick up a couple fish for the chowder, wearing
life jackets and paddling like crazy. Most of the day I spend at
the fire, baking bannock and catching up in my journal.

Last night the six of us stood around the fire in the damp and
drizzle and talked about what we're wanting and not getting
from each other, how we're angry, resentful, or insecure, how
two women's coupling off affects the rest of us. Nothing is
resolved, but I trust our willingness to keep working on it. We're
also in conflict about time. We're worried about reaching York
Factory on the 26th, and we differ on how important it is to do
it, how confident we feel, how to get going earlier. The problem
I think is that we're still partly on white man's time, needing
to meet a plane, a train, get back to jobs in the south. Otherwise,
I'd be fine with wherever we are.

In the evening I feel ill, take a nap, and dream about isolation
from the others. Then I dream a double rainbow across the lake.
I talk with Aurora about the dream and feel clearer. Moonrabbit
said this is a good time for me to be in touch with dreams, spir-

ituality. I had a powerful dream about Grammy—I think she may have died.

Jean hears women's voices singing in the rapids near this campsite. I've often heard women's voices in the wilderness, speaking quietly. She recalls legends of the sirens, of Rhine maidens.

In the morning a bear politely visits our camp and goes on her way.

DAY 17 BIGSTONE RIVER. RAPIDS. We're feeling a lot more confident, running more of the rapids than we thought we would. The river is getting bigger. Today started with an exciting bit of lining canoes through little waterfalls, an elaborate ferry system. ("Good," breathed Connie, "a group activity.") Very pleased with ourselves. Then at the next rapids we stalled out, and I got tense and irritable. Not runnable, not linable, no portage in sight. Not much energy in us. Finally we detected an ancient path (The James Fenimore Cooper Trail), reblazed it with the signs that mean "this trail, such as it is, brought to you courtesy of six Minnesota dykes on their way to the Bay," and doing that completely restored me to good humor. At the next rapids we took for the first time what seemed a deliberate and reasonable risk, first Kristin and I, then Kristin and Connie taking the loaded canoes through—by three different routes. In the middle of doing this we have to wait out a downpour. Huddled in our rainsuits we recall Farley Mowat's saying the Eskimos' clothes are their real dwellings, and patiently listen to the rain on the roof. Problems here are so solvable.

DAY 18 BIGSTONE RIVER. STOPPED. Aurora is sick—not just the familiar "camper's crud" runs, "going to visit the rabbits," but fever, hallucinations. Lorry is dosing her with belladonna from the homeopathic first aid kit. By the afternoon Aurora is weak but able to be up and join a group conference on whether we should try to push on with her as passenger, what's going on in our group dynamics, what we think the illness is about.

This has been building for days, and we spend the afternoon sitting in the sun in a difficult talk that ends with a lot more clarity and good feeling. Some new excitement too. Can we now possibly make it to York Factory by the 26th? We're all less confident, but more willing to give it a hell of a try. I'm feeling less mellow now, more eager, agreeing with Jean. I don't want to see us fail because of our own inertia. Does this push mean not taking time to connect with each other? No—in the city we need leisure, but here the bonding happens while working together. Are we too task-oriented, forgetting to have fun? We may have been misled into calling paddling work, the stopping fun, and that's not a distinction I feel. Maybe we're just starting to unlearn some city thinking. And we all will have to give up something—fishing time, photography time, lounging.

DAY 21 FOX RIVER. RUNNING THE RAPIDS. ROPING AND WADING. A good thing our talk brought us new energy because the trip is getting rougher. Two days ago Lorry and I went into a rapids feeling unconfident, stuck on a ledge, and I had to go for a swim to get us off. Angry at the others for not waiting. At the big burn we decided that walking was impossibly difficult in the pick-up-sticks tangle of logs and decided to rope, run, and hassle our way through a rapids we wouldn't have tried a few days ago.

The map-maker clearly travelled through in August, at low water levels. The Fox is getting very big, and the water level is very high. The power of it is awesome.

Today we came to what the map calls the most difficult part of the Fox. It starts with our picking our way through a maze of channels, getting stuck on a rock island with waterfalls all around us. The river drops out of sight ahead. We drag, rope, portage our canoes, then edge cautiously down the left bank until it makes us too nervous, and Connie finds a sort of portage. This one, unmarked on the map, is almost half a mile around heavy rapids, and ends below *five* parallel thirty-foot waterfalls across the wide river. "Freak-out Falls"—I mean, this one wasn't even mentioned. What's next?

Actually, I'm relieved. I've been feeling a lot of anxiety as the river gets bigger, gettting unclear—now that there's an objective cause for fear and the others share it, I relax, take on only my one-sixth of the responsibility. We cross the river in a terribly strong current, and I get my rapids nerve and judgment back leading around the inside of the bend.

And now we're 300 feet above sea level; in the last few days we've dropped 400 feet, sliding right off the Canadian Shield into the Hudson Bay lowlands. Last night we passed through a layer of beautiful red igneous rock, where four otters swam around us, snorting and laughing at us, running the rapids with us. Tonight we're below the rock, in the area of high clay banks. In the middle of that long brushy portage today we saw a beautiful mushroom in the middle of the trail, and after all the tromping back and forth it was still there, everyone having carefully stepped around it.

DAY 22 FOX RIVER. CAPSIZE CAMP. This was the day Kristin and Lorry capsized. This was what I'd feared since last winter—someone would capsize, I couldn't help them. We'd stopped to scout a bad place, and when we saw them appear below, out of the canoe, it was like a bad dream. Then we snapped out of it, and ran the notch we'd decided was too dangerous to go after them.

The whole thing worked out well, and we all got in on the rescue, Lorry calmly stuffing packs back into the canoe as she floated down the river, Kris and Lorry gallantly aiding each other, Aurora and I fishing them out of the river just above the next set of rapids, and finally Connie and Jean throwing ropes to get us all off the rocks where we'd managed to crash-land.

The last scene was pretty comic. Four of us and a canoe lodged on two tiny rocks, wild rapids around us, rain. By then we were all clearly safe, but it was complicated, and I felt absurdly cautious. We did this Marx sisters routine flinging ropes about, using the canoe as a ferry to get to an island. Does anyone remember how to tie a sheepshank? Connie watched her new paddle, dunked in the capsize, go spinning off down the river where Kris and Lorry didn't go, and called cheerily "Bye, sweetheart, and happy birthday."

The day was sobering, but in a pinch we found we were all there for each other, willing to take risks, competent. There's probably nothing we can't handle. Then we collected the other canoe, and paddled over to the portage to deal in our various styles with our fear, anger, relief, and a lot of wet gear.

DAY 24 FOX RIVER. HOME FREE. One last day of rapids, and Kristin and I wanted a chance to paddle together. (Moon had warned us we could escalate excitement, egg each other on.) We are all being very cautious now—Kris, subdued, warns us to keep lifejackets on while eating lunch in sight of the water. And still we get our chance at a rapids bigger than we'd have any right to choose to run. Scouting ahead, the two of us find ourselves in a place where, unless we wait for fall to lower the water level, our only choice is to run the rapids that we've just yelled to everyone else is out of the question. We wait for a potential rescue canoe to be lined to the bottom and then push off, and I'm afraid, but even more excited and pleased. Washing out at the bottom in a canoe half full of water I'm intensely joyful. This is what being alive and a dyke is all about. If I can just remember this moment clearly, I may never be afraid again.

DAY 26 HAYES RIVER AND YORK FACTORY. When we came out of the last rapids we had 120 miles to go and a plane that might be waiting for us in a day and a half. By evening there were only 90 miles left, and at the last campsite we cooked up most of the remaining food and started planning our strategy—four hours paddling, rest stops, another four hours, all day and night until we make it. We estimate 16 to 20 paddling hours. Is this crazy white man stuff? No. The plane doesn't have a lot to do with it any more—it's crazy, witchy, we just want to do it.

Just before dark the 25th we stop for dinner and make our flag—aluminum canoe-repair tape letters surround interlocked women's symbols: "We are everywhere." Partly for our friends back home. Then we paddle off into the dark. A beautiful yellow light ahead of us in the North, but otherwise it's too overcast to see a thing, and we navigate only by the largest islands.

Sometime in the middle of the night Aurora is too exhausted to go on. I keep falling asleep, but can hear Connie facilitating a discussion that gets us all what we want. Aurora and Lorry wrap up in sleeping bags and space blankets and bed down in the middle canoe; those of us who want to keep going tie our canoes up on either side and set off again. We make a very sluggish raft, and are paddling into a stiff cold headwind, but the current is still carrying us on. We start singing. Connie invents a lullaby for the occasion. I hardly look at Kristin in the stern of the other canoe, or say a word except as we steer off the sandbars, but we're comforted, knowing neither of us will ever quit.

Just before dawn she tells us we need to stop NOW to get warm. The wind off the Bay is icy, we're all numb, almost catatonic. We stumble out onto a dark beach and as the sun rises, realize how nearly hypothermic we are, what a task we've just finished. We put on every stitch of dry clothing, Aurora cooks us miso soup.

Paddling the last few miles into York Factory I'm very sleepy, very high. Intense sun and blue sky, cold wind, socks on my hands for mittens. Jean and I are paddling the flag ship, the orange flag is snapping around my head, and Jean still has to keep waking me up. I tell myself I may be missing the climax of the trip and then realize that whole idea of a climax is nonsense, and anyway, in my spacey sleepy state I'm soaking up impressions with my whole body. The permafrost-tipped trees are sliding past, mirages lie ahead where the river opens up, and I feel—how?—prayerful? Foggily I remember having felt that sometime before and then I remember it was on our first day. Now we've done this, and I don't really want to go back.

We finally seem to be there. Gunshots. The Indians are shooting at a polar bear out on the island. Doug, the caretaker of the historic site, is warm and welcoming, shows us where we can stay. We drag our gear up above the tideline and one by one fall asleep on the grass, wherever we happened to collapse. One by one we wake in a few minutes or hours and quietly start unpacking; Jean takes out the kite we've been carrying all this way and without a word goes out to fly it in celebration.

UNDATED NOTES. During the last week of the trip I started having paddling dreams, moving the tent downstream. Now after the trip Jean and Lorry and I all share the dream, paddling every night, all kinds of craft—motel rooms, housetrailers, our homes. It's always a dream of paddling at night, a profound body memory of those last miles.

My first day back in the city I get asthmatic, am very bummed out. Then I recover, remembering the way to handle this is not to block my senses and resist being here. For a while I walk around wearing moccasins, feeling alien to this culture but larger-than-lifesize and unbeatable.

A couple weeks after we return, four of us spend a week at a lesbian retreat—a new tribe, fourteen of us this time, talking about how to live our lives. Our expectations of ourselves and each other are so high it scares me. Sometimes we even live up to them.

One way we were that month only got clear to me later. We

didn't decide things by majority, of course, and often we didn't even use consensus. We simply knew who to listen to. And if the usual voice of caution, or caring, or whatever we needed wasn't heard, I knew one of the rest of us would say what was needed. Last spring I read a novel about the Pueblos, the council of elders who used silence as much as speech, waiting until they could move together, one voice speaking for them all. I was just beginning to hear our voices as less individual, more collective. I can't do that in the city, I find.

For a while after we returned we used "Hudson Bay" as a shorthand expression for a saner way of living. A "crazy trip" acquaintances sometimes say, but Aurora's back improved, Connie's ankle mended, I had no asthma, and we all returned strong and fit. And most of that time we all felt very safe. We talked of it often—an almost tangible sense of safety.

Women here think of the trip as dangerous. I'm in greater danger here every day. Only we can't afford to be aware of it, the randomness of violence, pointless deaths commuting to work, deaths of boredom and living by someone's rules. Up North there was a clarity, an environment that wasn't full of promises and lies. And an exhilaration in being able to take full responsibility for ourselves and each other.

NOTES ON CONTRIBUTORS

Ruth Baetz is the editor of *Lesbian Crossroads*, an interview book published by Morrow. She is a therapist in Seattle.

Sandy Boucher's stories and articles have appeared in many magazines. Two collections of her stories are *Assaults and Rituals* and *The Notebooks of Leni Clare*. Harper and Row published *Heartwoman*, her book of investigative/visionary pieces on Midwestern women. She is now working on a book about women and Buddhism.

Beth Brant was born in Detroit on May 6, 1941, of a Mohawk father and a white mother. Her clan is the Turtle, her number, Strength. Her Indian name, Degonwadonti, means "many opposed to one." She edited the special issue of *Sinister Wisdom* on North American Indian women. Her prose and poetry collection *Mohawk Trail* was published by Firebrand Books in 1985.

Sharon Budd, 41, is a lesbian mother of two daughters, Jackie, 17, and Jennie, 16. After completing an M.S. degree in counseling at the University of Kansas, she returned to the Pacific Northwest. She has been a housewife and a language teacher and has served in the Army.

Jeanne Cordova founded and published the *Lesbian Tide*. In thirty-five years, she has been a nun and a dyke. "Both vocations require living with and loving women for a lifetime. I have been blessed."

Margaret Cruikshank edited *Lesbian Studies* and *New Lesbian Writing*. She teaches gay and lesbian literature at the City College of San Francisco. She likes to walk on the beach and hike in the hills.

Rosemary Curb teaches English and women's studies at Rollins College in Florida. She lives with her daughter, Lisa. With Nancy Manahan she edited *Lesbian Nuns: Breaking Silence*.

Alix Dobkin lives in Preston Hollow, New York. In addition to *Lavender Jane*, she has made a record called *Living with Lesbians*.

Caroline Ferguson is an organizer who lives in Milwaukee. "Whenever possible, I am drawn to the vital out-of-doors of northern Wisconsin and the nourishment I find there."

Elsa Gidlow, born in Yorkshire, grew up in a French Canadian village on Montreal Island. Mainly self-educated, she was a poet-philosopher who lived for many years in northern California amid the redwoods. Her 1923 book *On a Gray Thread* was the first North American collection of poetry to celebrate love between women. Her anthology *Sapphic Songs: Eighteen to Eighty* is distributed by Naiad Press. Her autobiography *Elsa: I Come with My Songs* was published by Druid Heights Books and Booklegger Press shortly before her death in 1986.

Judy Grahn is one of the best-known poets of the women's movement. She edited a two-volume collection of short stories, *True to Life Adventure Stories*. Her book *Another Mother Tongue: Gay Words, Gay Worlds* combines history, philosophy and explorations of language. Her most recent work is *The Highest Apple: Sappho and the Lesbian Literary Tradition*.

Barbara Grier (Gene Damon) believes that a garden variety lesbian is resistant to blight. She has been collecting and reviewing lesbian literature for thirty years. One of the editors of *The Ladder*, she contributed to it regularly for sixteen years. She is now the editor of The Naiad Press, a feminist publishing company.

Susan Griffin is a poet (*Like the Iris of an Eye*) and a playwright (*Voices*) who lives in Berkeley with her daughter Becky. Her books *Woman and Nature: The Roaring Inside Her* and *Rape: The Power of Consciousness* were published by Harper and Row.

Jane Gurko is Associate Dean of Humanities at San Francisco State University, where she has taught English and women's studies since 1967. After she got tenure in 1973, she began to announce her lesbianism in the classroom, in writing, and in the community.

Monika Kehoe is working on a book on lesbians over sixty. Her poem "The San Andreas Fault" recently won a creative writing contest sponsored by the National Council on the Aging of Washington, D.C. In the original edition of *The Lesbian Path*, Dr. Kehoe used the pseudonym "Helen Trent" for the story of her early years and the pseudonym "Isabelle McTeigue" for the article about the government investigation of her in the 1950s.

Nancy Krody is Assistant Editor of the *Journal of Ecumenical Studies* at Temple University in Philadelphia. She and her spouse are remodeling a nine-room house. An ordained elder in the United Church of Christ, she serves as co-ordinator of the UCC Coalition for Gay Concerns. She edited *Genesis III*, a national ecumenical newsletter on women in religion, for four years. Her articles have appeared in *Foundations* and *Christianity and Crisis*.

Barbara Lightner is a lawyer and a member of the Board of Directors of the National Gay Task Force. Active in lesbian politics in Wisconsin, she is community action coordinator for the United, a gay group in Madison.

Audre Lorde lives on Staten Island and teaches at Hunter College. One of her eight books of poetry, *From a Land Where Other People Live*, was nominated for a National Book Award in 1974. Her most recent book of poetry is *Chosen Poems: Old and New*. Her autobiographical books are *Zami* and *The Cancer Journals*. She has also published *Sister Outsider: Essays and Speeches*.

Susan Madden is a feminist and sociologist who lives in Seattle.

Nancy Manahan, formerly an English teacher at Napa College, recently completed her Ph.D. at Columbia Pacific University. She is the co-editor of *Lesbian Nuns: Breaking Silence*. She owns a business with her partner in Napa.

Del Martin and **Phyllis Lyon** are two of the best known lesbian activists in the country. Together they wrote *Lesbian/Woman*, published in 1972, one of the first books to treat lesbianism from a feminist perspective. An updated version was published in 1983. Del has also written *Battered Wives* (1976).

Maree E. Martin was born in Brooklyn in 1943. She lived in Queens until 1972 and now lives in Louisville. In 1975 and 1976 she wrote for and performed with the Tampa Feminist Guerrilla Theater. Her poetry appears in *Drifts of Women's Minds* and *Womenspeak*.

DPat Mattie was born and raised in Mississippi, escaping at 17 by marrying an Air Force pilot. After years of military dependency and too much college, she set out at 35 to find herself. She now lives and writes in San Francisco. Her book of poetry *No Lies No More Not Now* was published in 1975.

Judith McDaniel was one of the founders of Spinsters, Ink, a feminist publishing company. Her publications include a monograph on Adrienne Rich; a poetry collection, *November Woman*; and a novel, *Winter Passage*. She chairs the literature Panel of the New York State Council on the Arts.

Cathie Nelson lives in Berkeley with her four children, her lover, and her lover's five children. She has a degree in women's studies from the University of California. She works as a computer programmer. In the original edition of *The Lesbian Path*, she wrote under the pseudonym Sarah Spencer.

Joan Nestle is a founding member of the Lesbian Herstory Archives in New York City and a teacher of third world studies. She lives with the memory of lost voices.

Judith Niemi has taught English for the University of Minnesota-Duluth and measured glaciers for McGill in the Arctic. A photographer, she is a founder of Woodswoman, a wilderness guide service in Minneapolis. She has written about Jane Rule for the lesbian issue of *Margins* and about herself for *The Coming Out Stories*.

Pat Parker is the author of five books of poetry: *Child of Myself, Pit Stop, Womanslaughter, Movement in Black,* and *Jonestown and Other Madness.* With Judy Grahn she made an album for Olivia Records titled *Where Would I Be Without You.*

Matile Poor is a university administrator and a therapist in San Francisco. She has led groups for lesbians over forty and lesbian mothers of teen-aged children. She has a Ph.D. in history from Columbia but in her next life wants to be a poet. The friend she writes about, Corky Wick, writes for Mothertongue Readers' Theater.

Minnie Bruce Pratt lives in Washington and teaches at the University of Maryland. She belonged to the collective that published *Feminary* for many years. She visits her boys at holidays and in the summer. Her publications include *The Sound of One Fork,* a collection of poetry, and essays on racism.

Ida VSW Red lives, loves, and works in San Francisco's Duboce Triangle, where she writes and performs with the feminist Mothertongue Readers' Theater; earns a living as a research librarian, editor, and writer; takes joy in a circle of creative woman-identified friends; and dreams of becoming a potent force for social change and the resurrection of women's rights.

Jane Rule is a novelist, reviewer and essayist who lives on Galiano Island off the coast of British Columbia. Writing fiction is her main occupation. Two of her recent collections of short stories are *The Outlander* and *Inland Passage.* Her biographical and critical study *Lesbian Images* was an early and important contribution to lesbian literature. Naiad Press recently published a collection of her essays, *A Hot-Eyed Moderate.*

May Sarton is one of the best-loved women writers in America. In the last ten years she has become recognized as a major writer. She has published numerous books of poetry, fiction, and autobiography, including *Journal of a Solitude* and *The House by the Sea.* Her novel *Mrs. Stevens Hears the Mermaids Singing* (1965) has a lesbian protagonist. *A World of Light* is both the title of a collection of sketches of her friends and relatives and the title of a movie made about her life and work.

Mitzi Simmons is a contributor to *Our Right To Love*.

Margaret Sloan-Hunter is a writer and activist who lives in Oakland. She and her daughter Kathy appear in a film about lesbian mothers, "In the Best Interests of the Children."

Other Grey Fox Books of Interest

John Coriolan	*Christy Dancing*
Daniel Curzon	*Human Warmth & Other Stories*
Patrick Franklin	*The Uncertainty of Strangers & Other Stories*
Robert Glück	*Elements of a Coffee Service*
Richard Hall	*Couplings, A Book of Stories*
	Letter from a Great-Uncle & Other Stories
	Three Plays for a Gay Theater
Claude Hartland	*The Story of a Life*
Eric Rofes	*"I Thought People Like That Killed Themselves"—Lesbians, Gay Men & Suicide*
Michael Rumaker	*A Day and a Night at the Baths*
	My First Satyrnalia
Samuel Steward	*Chapters from an Autobiography*
George Whitmore	*The Confessions of Danny Slocum*
Roy F. Wood	*Restless Rednecks: Gay Tales of a Changing South*
Allen Young	*Gays Under the Cuban Revolution*